JULIUS CÆSAR

The Players' Shakespeare

MACBETH

TWELFTH NIGHT

THE MERCHANT OF VENICE

KING HENRY IV PART ONE

A MIDSUMMER NIGHT'S DREAM

AS YOU LIKE IT

THE TEMPEST

HENRY V

ROMEO AND JULIET

ANTONY AND CLEOPATRA

HAMLET

OTHELLO

RICHARD II

Also edited by Dr J. H. Walter

HENRY V (Arden Shakespeare)

CHARLEMAGNE (Malone Society)

LAUNCHING OF THE MARY (Malone Society)

1599   Moved to Southwark near the Globe Theatre which he and his company had recently erected.

1602   Extensive purchases of property and land in Stratford.

1602–4   Lodged with Mountjoy, a Huguenot refugee and a maker of headdresses, in Cripplegate, London. Helped to arrange a marriage between Mary Mountjoy and Stephen Belott, her father's apprentice.

1603   His company became the King's Majesty's Players under royal patronage.

1607   His daughter Susanna married Dr John Hall.

1608   Birth of Shakespeare's grand-daughter Elizabeth Hall.

1610   Shakespeare possibly returned to live in Stratford.

1613   Purchase of the Gatehouse in Blackfriars. Burning of the Globe Theatre during the première of *Henry VIII*.

1616   Marriage of his daughter Judith to Thomas Quiney in Lent for which they were excommunicated.

25 March, 1616   Shakespeare altered the draft of his will presumably to give Judith more security in view of her husband's unreliability and his pre-marital misconduct with another woman. His will also revealed his strong attachment to his Stratford friends, and above all his desire to arrange for the establishment of his descendants.

23 April, 1616   Death of Shakespeare.

1623   Publication of the First Folio edition of Shakespeare's plays collected by his fellow actors Heminge and Condell to preserve 'the memory of so worthy a friend'.

JULIUS CÆSAR

Edited by

J. H. WALTER

M.A., PH.D.

Formerly Headmaster
Minchenden School, Southgate
Fellow of University College, London

HEINEMANN
EDUCATIONAL

Heinemann Educational
A Division of Heinemann Publishers (Oxford) Ltd
Halley Court, Jordan Hill, Oxford OX2 8EJ
OXFORD   LONDON   EDINBURGH
MADRID   ATHENS   BOLOGNA   PARIS
MELBOURNE   SYDNEY   AUCKLAND
IBADAN   NAIROBI   HARARE   GABORONE
SINGAPORE   TOKYO   PORTSMOUTH NH (USA)

ISBN 0 435 19003 2

93 94 95 96 24 23 22 21 20

Printed in England by Clays Ltd, St Ives plc

CONTENTS

PREFACE   *page* 1

INTRODUCTION   3

JULIUS CÆSAR   29

APPENDICES:

    I   The Sources of *Julius Cæsar*   208
   II   Shakespeare's Theatre   211

PREFACE

THE aim of this edition is to encourage pupils to study the play as a play, to see it not so much as a novel or a historical narrative, but as a pattern of speech and movement creating an artistic whole. This approach stimulates and enlivens classroom work and is also a most fruitful way of preparing for examinations.

The interleaved notes, therefore, contain, in addition to a gloss, interpretations of character, dialogue and imagery, considered particularly from the point of view of a play. There are some suggestions for acting, for the most part simple pointers to avoid rigidity of interpretation and drawn up with an apron stage in mind. Some questions are interposed to provide topics for discussion or to assist in discrimination.

It is suggested that the play should be read through rapidly with as little comment as possible. On a second reading the notes should be used in detail, and appropriate sections of the Introduction might be read at the teacher's discretion.

It is hoped that this edition will enable teachers to take the class more deeply into the play than the usual meagre allowance of time permits them to do; it is not an attempt to usurp their function.

The play was not published before the First Folio edition, 1623, which is the basis of all subsequent texts. Other editions have been consulted, and of the modern editions those by C. J. Sisson, J. Dover Wilson, G. L. Kittredge, T. S. Dorsch (Arden, 1955) have proved most helpful. The text is complete. Stage directions follow in the main those of the Folio which was probably printed from the playhouse prompt-copy. The locations of scenes added by previous editors have been placed in the notes. The notes make no reference to anachronisms.

Among the many books that contain studies of *Julius Cæsar* the following have been particularly useful, and I have gratefully drawn on them:

H. Granville Barker, *Prefaces to Shakespeare, Vol. II*, 1958; A. Bonjour, *The Structure of Julius Cæsar*; G. Wilson Knight, *The Imperial Theme*;

1

Preface

M. W. MacCallum, *Shakespeare's Roman Plays*; R. G. Moulton, *Shakespeare as a Dramatic Artist*; C. J. Sisson, *New Readings in Shakespeare*; D. A. Stauffer, *Shakespeare's World of Images*; B. Stirling, *Unity in Shakespearian Tragedy*; V. Whitaker, *Shakespeare's Use of Learning*.

Similarly I am indebted to articles in periodicals by R. A. Foakes, L. Kirschbaum, L. C. Knights, E. Schanzer, B. Stirling and R. W. Zandvoort.

J.H.W.

INTRODUCTION

i

ON 21st September 1599, Thomas Platter, a Swiss traveller, recorded that he saw a play in London:

> After lunch . . . at about two o'clock, I and my party crossed the river, and there in the house with the thatched roof we saw an excellent performance of the tragedy of the first Emperor *Julius Cæsar* with about fifteen characters; after the play according to their custom they did a most elegant and curious dance, two dressed in men's clothes, and two in women's.

There is no doubt that the play he saw was Shakespeare's *Julius Cæsar*, and the theatre was probably the Globe which was built earlier that year. *Julius Cæsar* therefore was one of the first plays to be performed at the Globe, and from other evidence it was almost certainly written earlier in 1599, perhaps immediately after *Henry V*.

Shakespeare was always attracted by the story of Julius Cæsar even in jest as the 'hook-nosed fellow of Rome', but more often as the great man

> whose remembrance yet
> Lives in men's eyes, and will to ears and tongues
> Be theme and hearing ever (*Cymbeline,* III. i, 2–4)

He was also profoundly concerned by the theme of political assassination and the miseries of rebellion and civil war; which he had repeatedly explored in previous plays. The anxious political

3

situation in 1599, the urgent need to establish the succession to the throne, the constant threat of rebellion and of assassination of the aged queen, the ominous, unpredictable posturings of the Earl of Essex, would have made the story of the murder of the greatest figure in Rome particularly topical and perhaps a timely parable. For Heywood, a fellow dramatist, pointed out that the aim of history plays was to instruct their hearers in obedience to the throne, and to correct their vices by displaying the untimely ends of rebels and evil doers. Indeed, the story had already been used as a warning. Bynneman's introductory epistle to his translation (1578) of Appian's *Civil Wars* stated: 'How God plagueth them that conspire againste theyr Prince, this Historie declareth at the full. For of all them that coniured against *Caius Cæsar,* not one did escape violent death. The which this Author hathe a pleasure to declare, bycause he would affray all men from disloyalte toward their soueraigne.' The slight but clear resemblances between the characteristics Shakespeare has given Cæsar, apart from what he found in his source, and some well-known characteristics of Elizabeth may delicately hint at a significant parallel.

It is perhaps too much to suggest, however tempting, the more commercial motive, namely, that Elizabeth's translation of Plutarch's essay 'On Curiosity', which occupied her leisure in November 1598, came to Shakespeare's knowledge, and that he sought to appeal to the royal taste for Plutarch by dramatizing one of the *Lives* (see Appendix I).

Whatever the motives the tragedy of the ruler of the world was a magnificent, impressive and not inapt play with which to celebrate the opening of the Globe (i.e. the World). If it was not the first play acted there, it was almost certainly the first tragedy.

II

POPULARITY AND INTERPRETATIONS

The play was popular. It was frequently quoted soon after its appearance, an indication of the impressive impact it had made.

An interesting comment on the play by Digges, in a commend-atory poem probably intended for inclusion in the First Folio, shows how enthralled the spectators were by the quarrel scene— a scene that some later writers have considered dramatically irrelevant—

> So I have seen, when Cæsar would appear,
> And on the stage at half-sword parley were,
> *Brutus* and *Cassius*: oh how the audience
> Were ravish'd, with what wonder they went thence.

The Admiral's company of actors, rivals to Shakespeare's company, perhaps envious of the success of *Julius Cæsar,* paid them the compliment of commissioning a play, *Cæsar's Fall,* in 1602.

Certainty about the interpretation of the play has given place in recent times to doubt and puzzlement. Is it a history play, a tragedy, or a revenge play? Is Cæsar or Brutus the villain? Are they both tragic heroes? As one critic has written: 'Yet though Brutus is the actual and visible hero, it is not at all far-fetched to say . . . that the spiritual hero is the "great daemon" of Cæsar.' Is its theme the history of a rebellion, liberty versus tyranny, the old order against the new, republicanism versus absolute monarchy, private life versus public life, Rome, or Cæsar's revenge?

Yet there is considerable agreement on the excellence of the play. 'This play is a masterpiece of Elizabethan stagecraft'; '. . . perhaps the most brilliant and most penetrating artistic reflection of political realities in the literature of the world'; 'there is no rival in modern drama to this vivid and truthful evocation of the Roman spirit in action.' It is also hailed not only as a turning point in Shakespeare's career, a bridge between the history plays and the tragedies leading directly on to *Hamlet*, but as a landmark in the history of English tragedy.

Shakespeare clearly took great care over the play. Its style is bare and direct, possessing elegance and restraint. The minor characters, economically sketched, come vividly to life. The

effort of historical imagination that produced so brilliant a reconstruction of Roman character is remarkable. His detailed handling
of his source material shows the most careful and ingenious
modulations to achieve an effect rather different from that given
by Plutarch. In short, as a recent editor writes: 'No other of
Shakespeare's plays is so perfectly written, its verse so studiously
attuned, for the characters who are to speak its lines and for its
setting'.

Some characteristics of the play deserve further comment.

It has no sub-plot and hardly any comic element (for the comedy
of the citizens has a grim edge to it), nothing to distract attention
from the main plot or the prevailing tone. The main characters
give the impression of maturity if not middle age, and show little
sign of a sense of humour.

The portents, omens, dreams and ghostly visitations that
shadow the chief characters are not mere attempts to create an
appropriate atmosphere. The Elizabethan conception of the
divine order of the universe linked the heavens with the body of
the state and with the body of man, so that events in the heavens
were thought to influence and correspond with events in both
states and individuals. Eclipses, meteors, comets were disorderly
events in the heavens, and therefore inevitably heralded disorder
on earth and within the mind of man. Although there were
sceptics, the Elizabethans would see in the presentation of the
storm and its prodigies a warning of disasters and calamities to be
visited upon men, pagan or christian, by God. Indeed some of the
very prodigies mentioned by Calphurnia and Casca, and the
typical attitude of mind occur in Batman's book, *Doom Warning
All Men to the Judgement*, 1581. Had not the terrible storm on the
eve of Essex' departure for Ireland correctly forecast the failure of
the expedition? Men disregarded such things at their peril out of
folly or pride.

Cæsar, pious though he is as becomes a great ruler, brushes them
aside out of over-confidence or because his vanity is touched by

Decius. Brutus, exposed to the prodigies in his orchard (is there any other reason for this scene to take place in the open air and not under shelter?) is unaware of their influence on him, an influence made clear to the audience by his description of the disorder and insurrection within him. Cassius sees the portents as a challenge, and misconstrues them as a warning against the assumption of the crown by Cæsar. Both Brutus and Cassius are compelled by the forces they have loosed to accept against their beliefs the truth of omens and ghostly visitations. For Cassius, his jeer at Cæsar's new-found superstition has come full circle. The supernatural, cosmic theme presents the detached spectators with the sharp savour of the ironies of circumstance in which the characters play out their destinies.

Brutus, seeking to dignify the murder of Cæsar, proposes to 'carve him as a dish fit for the gods', to make a rite or ceremony of the killing. The assumed reverence in the conspirators' approach to Cæsar, the kneeling, kissing his hand and falling prostrate, and the ceremonial washing of hands in Cæsar's blood fulfil the pattern of Brutus' intention. Stirling suggests that the arrival of Antony's servant with words that echo those of the conspirators—'kneel', 'fall', 'prostrate', introduces the mockery of a counter-ritual, which Antony continues by the elaborate hand-shaking, the stressing of the deer, carcass and butchers image (previously rejected by Brutus), the prophecy of civil strife, and a detailed account of the treacherous stab-wounds. Antony effectively destroys Brutus' conception of the assassination even before the events in the market place; the sacrifice to the gods was not accepted.

More than one writer has called attention to the strong love-element in the play, a net of love embraces all the main characters except the aloof Octavius. Brutus is greatly loved by all who know him from Cæsar and Portia down to his servant and his soldiers. He responds in love to all, but violates his bond of love with Cæsar. Some consider that this ruthless destruction of love diminishes Brutus, atrophies his capacity for love and leads to his disaster. Cassius deeply loves Brutus and subdues his will to him. Antony's passionate love for Cæsar impels him to avenge the murder. Brutus who had rejected love ironically reconciles himself to dying with the knowledge of the constant love of his friends, a consolation he had treacherously denied to Cæsar.

The persistent tradition of the morality plays has left its mark on *Julius Cæsar*. Cassius' soliloquy (I. ii, 302–9) intrudes on the relationship between himself and Brutus. Up to this point Cassius has uttered to his close friend Brutus a fierce denunciation of Cæsar and has urged Brutus to save Rome. Now it all proves to have been a piece of Vice-like intrigue to ensnare Brutus; a view which is echoed later (I. iii, 154–6). The pattern extends further. Portia and Lucius, it has been suggested, have something of the function of good angels, or Virtues. Lucius, his name associated with the symbolism of light in the play, has significant actions in his appearances and withdrawals twice to sleep during periods of Brutus' surrender to the conspirators and the visitation of Cæsar's spirit. Both of them have left Brutus before his death at Philippi, Portia by suicide, and Lucius is not heard of after the visitation of Cæsar's spirit at Sardis. Brutus is faced with a moral choice, the theme of morality plays. However, his struggle is not represented in full by formal, external allegory, it is subtly reflected by Lucius' taper and instrument, and by Portia's care for Brutus' sick soul. Brutus' soliloquies show his inner struggle and his false choice following his faulty reasoning. It is this latter technique that Shakespeare develops most effectively in the later tragedies.

The crowd's fickleness and its susceptibility to mass emotions have been frequently stressed, but the ominous undertones of its threat to stable government in I. i appear to have escaped notice. The cobbler's jests on 'mend' and 'awl' are not merely to tickle the ears of the groundlings. 'Mend-all' was the name by which Jack Cade, the rebel, was widely known, and it was frequently referred to by Shakespeare's contemporaries when they denounced disaffected, rebellious commoners.

III

CÆSAR

Most editors and critics, rejecting the testimony of Brutus, Cassius, and Antony that Cæsar is 'the foremost man of all this world', that he 'bear the palm alone', and was the 'heart of the world', 'the noblest man that ever lived in the tide of times', find Cæsar if not a caricature of greatness at least senile, superstitious, and boastful, and are puzzled at the dramatic impropriety of such a figure. Even those who accept Cæsar's greatness as established by the comment of others and by Cæsar's utterances and actions, are at a loss to account for apparently contradictory aspects of his character.

The following statements, phrases, epithets from various writers show the trend of condemnation of Cæsar: strutting piece of puff-paste, glorious vapourer and braggart, trembling epileptic, credulous, vacillating, infatuated with his own greatness, senile, ranting shadow, Roman Tamburlaine of illimitable ambition and ruthless irresistible genius, monstrous tyrant, ludicrous, pompous, opposing to the first falterings of the mind an increasingly rigid and absolute assertion of the Cæsar idea.

Cæsar's admirers are not so eloquent: courteous host, courageous, constant (in statecraft), penetrating judge of his fellow men, sensitive to public opinion, ideal governor, tender husband, one of the master spirits of mankind, practical, has force and strength of character, impressive, dignified, complete in all the greatness that belongs to action, unshaken, unseduced, unterrified, builds above his weaknesses the conception of the impersonal Cæsar.

Various attempts have been made to explain or reconcile these character differences. Shakespeare, it is said, deliberately worte Cæsar down 'for some dramatic reason or other', or, in order 'to write Brutus up'. Again, Shakespeare is portraying the divergen-

cies between the public figure and the private man. He is stressing
Cæsar's physical shortcomings so that the power of his spirit may
appear the greater, or so that he may not tower over the other
characters and destroy the dramatic balance, or so that the conspirators may be provided with some semblance of justification
for the murder. From another angle it has been suggested that the
ambiguities in Cæsar's character were a deliberate dramatic
device, for by playing on the opposing views of the Cæsar story
—justly killed tyrant or foully murdered great prince—current in
his audience Shakespeare induced dramatic suspense.

Dorsch (Arden 1955) finds much to admire in Cæsar's character. Among other things he denies that Cæsar is superstitious:
he disregards the soothsayer and the portents; the cure for
barrenness and the appeal to the augurers would be normal
among Romans. Nor is Cæsar vacillating, he is momentarily
swayed by Calphurnia's distressed entreaties; rather is he foolhardy and boastful in this scene. His susceptibility to flattery and
his arrogance are of little importance except when the latter
alienates sympathy from him just before the murder.

Three further points of interpretation which do not seem to
have been mentioned before are added for consideration. Cæsar,
at his first appearance in what an Elizabethan would have recog-
nized as the official showing-forth ceremony on the day preceding a coronation, shows not only reverence for a religious
festival and for his ancestors, but also through Calphurnia he
participates in it. At the same time as a possible king-elect he
displays a proper anxiety to secure the succession, a matter of
great concern to the audience, subjects of the unmarried Elizabeth.
On the morning after the storm he seeks divine guidance from
the priests, guidance which he is foolhardy enough to reject, as he
had done the warning of the soothsayer. Is Cæsar in fact not a
superstitious man, but a pious man, a qualification considered
necessary in a great leader? Henry V's piety and request for
guidance from the prelates is a similar instance. Of course Cassius

says he is superstitious—and Cassius is an honourable man!

Cæsar's speech, III. i, 58–73, is regarded as a piece of boastful arrogance that invites retribution by the gods, and dramatically saves the murder from being mere brutal butchery. But is it that entirely? Cæsar has just entertained a few friends with wine before they escort him to the Capitol. There they besiege him with pleas to waive a decree of banishment. Cæsar, disgusted to find these so-called friends crawling in nauseating fashion to beg him to tamper with the law, angrily rebuffs them. He feels that he himself is the only upright and constant man in a corrupt world of knaves and flatterers, and this emotion gives his words their over-emphasis.

It has been noted that many of Cæsar's characteristics are Shakespeare's invention, but it has not apparently been noted that many of these are also characteristics of Queen Elizabeth I. She was given to swooning under the pressure of strong emotions, and she had an almost pathological dislike of bad smells (compare I. ii, 245–6). Her vacillation was notorious (compare II. ii, 105–7). When her household was alarmed for her safety on the appearance of the comet of 1583, she adopted an attitude like that of Cæsar (II. ii, 26–7) and uttered words spoken by him on another occasion, 'Jacta est alea'. In her later years she was revered as almost divine under the symbolism of the goddess Diana or Cynthia (compare I. ii, 115–16, 121). In 1599 she was ageing, frail and arrogant, but there was no doubt of the power of her spirit. Was Shakespeare complimenting her by using her as a model of greatness of spirit, was he reflecting the tense political situation of the time and perhaps giving a warning to would-be rebels, or was he doing both or neither?

IV

BRUTUS

As a complement to the unfavourable view which is frequently taken of Cæsar, Brutus has received much praise. The characters in the play speak well of him—except perhaps Artemidorus. Brutus even speaks well of himself. Integrity, humility, courtesy, consideration (for servants), sincerity, morality, virtue, courage, lovableness, stoicism, chivalry, honour, fortitude are all good qualities that have been attributed to him. On the other hand weaknesses or flaws in his character have been noted: pride, divided mind, frigidity, conceit, arrogance, boastfulness, self-deception, naivety, muddleheadedness, folly, priggishness, egotism, more loved than loving, opinionated. Two critical opinions summarize the position: Brutus believes in an ideal, honour, but confuses it with treachery; Brutus is a man whose motive we can respect even if we cannot understand it.

Hotspur's career in *1 Henry IV* shows that when honour is in question, reason and judgement disappear leaving, among other things, a man vulnerable to suggestion. Troilus (*Troilus and Cressida*, II. ii, 47–50) puts the matter clearly:

> manhood and honour
> Should have hare hearts, would they but fat their thoughts
> With this crammed reason; reason and respect
> Make livers pale and lustihood deject.

Brutus, already uneasy in mind and thus fit for the Vice-like ingenuity of Cassius, proudly proclaims his devotion to honour. Cassius takes this quality which Brutus regards as supreme and unassailable as a weakness through which he gulls Brutus (I. ii, 92, 304–6). It is not therefore surprising to find Brutus, further confused under the baleful meteors, attempting to justify the murder he proposes. Throughout the play his judgement is woefully at fault, and again he is gulled, this time by Antony. Once committed to the plot he is involved in deceit and dissimulation (II. i, 224–5), though once his heart misgives him (II. ii, 128–9). But is his action in kissing Cæsar's hand (III. i, 52) a tender farewell or a Judas-betrayal?

He assumes the leadership of the conspirators, and immediately displays self-deception and a lack of imaginative awareness. He proposes to spiritualize the murder as a ritual sacrifice to purge Rome, and out of his rigid uprightness and obtuseness discounts the prudent practical suggestions of the others. He will not consider the influential Cicero as an accomplice, but only the ailing Ligarius. What too is the condition of his mind that he insists on the murderers bathing their hands in Cæsar's blood? Its intention is to share the responsibility for the murder and perhaps to maintain the ritual aspect, yet is it a dignified inspiring gesture or 'a savage spectacle' that shakes the mind? His honest acceptance of responsibility and complacent innocence lead to his naive and pathetic undertaking to speak to the crowd before Antony.

The quarrel scene reveals Brutus slowly stripped of his illusions, and he is forced into attitudes ironically like those of the man he had murdered. His action has brought proscriptions to Rome, Cassius and his fellows are ready to condone practices for which Cæsar was condemned, Portia has committed suicide, and the ghost of Cæsar warns him of death. Under the stress he is irritable, unfair, arrogant, and eventually breaks down (IV. iii, 144). It is the only occasion on which he retracts an opinion. After the reconciliation he recovers poise and strength to greet the ghost with fortitude.

In the last scenes aware of guilt (V. v, 50) and his philosophy destroyed by circumstance, the love he inspires in others comes to his comfort, and Antony's epitaph buries 'all unkindness'. His very virtues which Cassius thought essential to the success of the plot ironically proved its undoing; murder even though it aims at killing the spirit is never an abstraction.

V

ANTONY

Comment on Antony has followed closely what Plutarch said about him. In the *Lives* though he is acknowledged to be a good soldier, open-handed, and popular with his men, yet he is unjust, insolent and given to drunken feasts, dancing and plays; and in the 'Comparison with Cleon' that follows the 'Life of Antony' Plutarch states that Antony's acts after Cæsar's death were done out of desire for personal gain. The following epithets and phrases have been applied to him: unprincipled, resourceful, bold, ambitious of honour and power, unscrupulous, vicious, remorseless, opportunist, a voluptuary, a demagogue of the most profligate description, an artist, a politician, no sense of moral obligation.

In the first two scenes Antony takes little part in affairs. Cæsar teases him for his late night revelry, and after he has run the course, discusses Cassius with him; Brutus dismisses him as 'quick-spirited' and a 'limb of Cæsar' useless by itself; Cassius calls him a 'shrewd contriver' and is uneasy about him. After the murder Antony reveals a love for Cæsar that is real and deep; there is no evidence to substantiate a charge of 'unmitigated self-seeking'. His soliloquy—and soliloquies in Shakespeare's plays reveal the truth of the speaker's mind—pleads forgiveness for the necessity of feigning friendship with the murderers, and proclaims the curse of civil war and revenge for the foul deed. The speech is similar in purpose and style to the Bishop of Carlisle's protesting prophecy in *Richard II*, IV. i, 136–49. The phrases he uses when there is no need to dissemble—'butchers', 'foul deed', 'cruel issue of these bloody men', and his tears (III. i, 282–5) testify to the genuineness of his love for Cæsar and his hatred of the murderers, who themselves are not innocent of dissembling while accepting their victim's hospitality. Whether one regards his feelings as sincere or not, his handling of the conspirators and his oration to the citizens are a work of genius; he overthrows the conspirators and at the same time restores the greatness, nobility and fame of Julius Cæsar.

For many the grim proscription scene damns Antony and shows his ruthless brutality, which the later news of the wholesale executions of the senators does nothing to diminish. Then too, he diverts money from Cæsar's legacies, presumably to support the cost of forces to be used against Brutus and Cassius. There is no escaping the ruthlessness of the proscriptions, even though Octavius and Lepidus start the bargaining over the lives of kinsmen, and even though they are surrounded by enemies and cannot tell friend from foe. As for the money Antony's action is somewhat less corrupt than the activities of Cassius' 'itching palm'. Antony's proposal to use and then to throw aside the 'slight unmeritable' Lepidus is unscrupulous scheming. He is involved in three matters similar in kind to those faced by Brutus; his actions are in complete contrast and are balanced against those of Brutus. He does not restrict the number of deaths, he uses any man, however unworthy, to achieve his purpose, and he has no scruples about appropriating money bequeathed apparently to the citizens. Brutus it will be remembered, restricts the killing to Cæsar, he refuses to use Cicero and Antony, and he refuses to wring money from the peasants by 'indirection'.

In the meeting between the opponents before the battle at Philippi his love for Cæsar occasions his outburst against the hypocritical actions of Brutus and Cassius. In battle he is calm and generous to the captured Lucilius; in victory he is magnanimous towards the dead Brutus.

VI

CASSIUS

Cæsar's brilliant sketch of Cassius is the basis for any study of his character and significance, but it leaves much out, particularly the qualities that predominate in the last two acts. In his first appearance Cassius' envy of Cæsar, his bitter hostility towards Cæsar's authority and power mark him as the type of stage-character known to the Elizabethans as the 'malcontent', an ominous, brooding opponent of existing society. Cæsar's description confirms this. A further twist is given in his soliloquy where in the tradition of the morality play Vice he announces his intention of seducing Brutus.

His emotions determine his political sympathies. Hating Cæsar he fails to see the power of Cæsar's spirit and any virtue in absolute rule. His single-minded blindness leads him to mis-interpret the portents and omens, and to fail to foresee the effect of inviting Brutus to lead the conspiracy. He is a materialist, and though he talks of the freedom of the spirit, his actions and suggestions are practical and expedient.

In the quarrel scene it is clear that he has not grasped the high purpose which led Brutus to the assassination of Cæsar. As the scene progresses, he is the more concerned at the thought of losing Brutus' love—he had shown a similar concern at the outset of the play when he misunderstood Brutus' aloofness. The abuse Brutus hurls at him—'rash choler', 'madman', 'choleric', 'testy humour', 'venom of your spleen', 'waspish'—hardly seems to be justified by Cassius' words; Brutus is the more waspish of the two. Cassius' passionate offer to give his heart moves Brutus in love to set aside his principles, 'Do what you will, dishonour shall be humour'. Neither of them can do without love, in that is their reconciliation sealed. His friendship smothers his better judge-ment in accepting Brutus' counsel to march on Philippi. Fey under the influence of the omens he enters the battle in good heart, fiercely kills his standard-bearer for cowardice, mistakes the greeting of Titinius and impetuously commands Pindarus to kill him. The 'last of all the Romans' is Brutus' tribute; the sad reproach of Titinius is perhaps near the truth, 'Alas, thou hast misconstrued everything'.

VII

ELIZABETHAN STAGE PRACTICE AND THE PLAY

The stage conditions described in Appendix II determined to a large extent the shape of the plays, their dramatic devices, their methods and conventions.

Introduction

The general lack of scenery gave the dramatist freedom to shift the scene of his play as often as he liked (*Antony and Cleopatra* has thirteen scenes in Act III), to change the scene unannounced while the actors remained on the stage (*Twelfth Night*, III. iv, begins in Olivia's orchard and ends in the street) or following an announcement (*Julius Cæsar*, III. i, 11–12; IV. ii, 51), or, where knowledge of locality was not necessary for the understanding of the plot, to place it nowhere in particular, or in a place inconsistent with an earlier statement (IV. i). Quarto and Folio editions are not introduced with any statement of where they take place, and some scenes do not require it. The precise locating of every scene would distract attention from the plot; the scene is where the actors are. Such imprecision coupled with the rapid two-hour flow of the play uninterrupted by breaks for scene or costume changes helped to maintain the dramatic spell.

There are some points of doubt about the staging of *Julius Cæsar*. In III. i, 11–12 it is unlikely that Cæsar would move from the outer stage to the small discovery space, or inner chamber as representing the Capitol. He may have moved from the outer part of the stage to that part under the canopy. Alternatively and more likely his procession may have come from the yard of the theatre and mounted the side of the platform which then represented the Capitol. In a similar manner the citizens may have mounted and passed 'over the stage' at the beginning of I. i. The peculiar stage directions at V. ii and V. iv whereby Brutus and Messala re-enter in battle array the stage they have just left may also imply action between these scenes and the preceding scenes involving entry in force from the yard (see *Shakespeare Survey* 12 (1959), pp. 47–55). Another suggestion is that the use of 'mansions' or 'tents', as at IV. ii, 51, may mean that the actors did not leave the stage. An interesting sign of Shakespeare's care in this play is the large number of stage directions embodied in the text.

The stage balcony was presumably used for the hill to which Pindarus is sent at V. iii, 20.

There was a similar freedom in the treatment of time. Inevitably some scenes overlapped, but Shakespeare placed scenes out of their chronological order, he foreshortened time, or sometimes he merely obscured it. Flavius and Marullus are apparently 'put to silence' within a few minutes of their 'disrobing the images' (I. ii, 279–80). When Brutus found time to give Ligarius reasons (II. i, 219) is not clear, he was still doubtful of his intentions at I. iii, 154–6 and at the beginning of II. i. The concern is not with the orderly sequence of events in real life, but with the illusion of time in a play. No mention is made of the lapse of time between III. iii and IV. i, or between IV. i and IV. ii and iii, or between IV. iii and V. i; the events appear to crowd swiftly on each other driving on remorselessly to the tragic ending. Yet Shakespeare by precise and frequent marking of the time builds up an atmosphere of tension and suspense in the scenes leading up to Cæsar's murder (II. i, 2–3, 103–4, 192, 213, 221; II. ii, 114, 121; II. iv, 23).

The plays at the Theatre and the Globe took place in the afternoon and daytime was assumed in their action. Night was mentioned directly or by reference to torches, candles, or lanterns if the action demanded it as in *A Midsummer Night's Dream*, II. i, or as in *Macbeth*, to help create an atmosphere of horror and evil.

An important convention was the practice of the soliloquy and the aside. The jutting out of the stage into the middle of the theatre floor brought the actors who were well forward nearer to the bulk of the audience than to actors at the rear of the stage. It had long been established that character and motives were announced directly, the audience was not left to guess what was going on in a character's mind. It was a simple matter, therefore, for an actor to come forward out of earshot of the others on the stage and reveal confidentially to the audience his character, his motives and his intentions. In this way Shylock declared his villainy, Cassius his intention to seduce Brutus, and Brutus his agonizing inner struggle. This device linked actor and audience intimately: the spectators shared in the play, they had a god-like knowledge of the hearts of the characters, and the two things increased their feelings of tension and suspense and the moments of dramatic irony. The aside, a brief pointed remark, was often ironic, or it gave the audience a kind of nudge to remind them of some matter. It too sustained the sense of intimacy between actor and audience.

Disguising, unconvincing though it may seem, was an accepted convention. Shakespeare in other plays made considerable use of heroines disguised in male dress, a device made easy by the employment of boy actors for female parts. Here there is the pretence by Lucilius that he is Brutus, hardly a true form of disguising, but a ruse to allow Brutus time to rejoin other parts of his army.

The ornate stage, the magnificent costumes (the principal actors may have worn Roman costume in spite of references to Cæsar's nightshirt and doublet, and to the conspirators' cloaks), the royal and noble characters produced an element of formal pageantry in the performance of the plays. Gesture and stage business were formal, dignified and restricted, and the emphasis was placed on the delivery of the speeches. To an audience accustomed to the impressive oratory of preachers at St. Paul's Cross, to sustained and eloquent speaking by its notabilities trained in rhetoric, the words of a play were particularly important. A well-spoken passage of rich word-painting reporting, for example, some event that had happened off stage was rousing and satisfying. It was a kind of pageantry in speech or as a Jacobean writer put it, 'an ampullous and scenicall pomp' of words.

VIII

VERSE AND PROSE

The impact of dialogue was enhanced by its traditional verse form; it gave to the major characters an impressive grandeur, a stature larger than life. In Shakespeare's plays its range, power and flexibility are truly astounding, and he contrasts it from time to time with passages of prose almost as varied in style and form.

Shakespeare's verse is infinitely varied. He uses heroic couplets to form a stately narrative verse in *Richard II,* or two speakers can each speak a line of a couplet the second speaker making a comment on the first (*A Midsummer Night's Dream,* I. i, 196–201). A few couplets appearing in blank verse may mark an intense emotion; a single couplet may mark a wise or significant saying, or an important exit. Couplets can impart a sense of finality, of steps taken from which there can be no turning back. Couplets of shorter lines, however, are often mocking jingles (*Merchant of Venice,* I. i, 111–12) though they too can be impressively final (*A Midsummer Night's Dream,* V. i, 404 ff.). In this play there are very few couplets even at the end of scenes where we may expect them. Cassius in soliloquy ends I. ii with a couplet threatening Cæsar, Artemidorus rhymes his concluding lines (II. iii, 13–14), Brutus ends V. iii with a resolution to fight again, and the play ends with a formal couplet. Titinius ends his valediction on Cassius with a couplet expressing his sense of doom (V. iii, 63–4), and both Titinius and Brutus die with a couplet on their lips. Does this notable absence of couplets suggest that Shakespeare was not in a 'rhyming vein', or that he thought couplets were inconsistent with a Roman style, or that the staging of the play, probably with a free use of 'mansions', made couplets unnecessary as warnings?

In early plays such as *Love's Labour's Lost* and *Romeo and Juliet* Shakespeare used elaborate rhyme patterns. The first words Romeo and Juliet speak to each other form the pattern of a sonnet. Such patterns employed with elaborate figures of speech are a sign of the depth and sincerity of the speakers' feelings. We are inclined to regard them as artificial and insincere, but to an Elizabethan they truly reflected the strength and complexity of the emotion described. No such devices are used in this play. The dignity and epic nature of tragedy and history plays is alien to the lyrical forms that express romantic love.

Shakespeare's blank verse can be elaborate, enriched with swiftly following metaphors, with similes and other figures of speech or tricks of style, and with mythological allusions; it can be plain and direct; or it can become exaggerated and violent in language in the description of warfare, in frenzied appeals to the heavens, and in boasting. Its rhythms can march with regular beat, or, particularly in later plays like *King Lear* and *Antony and Cleopatra*, the rhythms are infinitely varied to achieve the most subtle effects. The characters may use the kind of blank verse appropriate to the dramatic moment and not necessarily the kind consistent with what is known of them elsewhere in the play. Why do the citizens who speak in prose in I. i use verse of a kind in III. ii?

Thus Cassius normally speaks direct discursive and narrative verse occasionally in his tirades deepened and compacted by tersely expressed thought (I. ii, 135–41; indeed I. iii, 89–102, including two spoken by Casca, have almost a sonnet movement). Yet his powerful emotions shorten his sentences and make him utter impassioned jets of speech (I. iii, 108–15; IV. iii, 92–106).

Brutus' verse is the vehicle for meditation and argument and is consequently well-ordered, smooth and controlled (II. i, 10–34; II. i, 114–40); occasionally it is charged with images as he develops the emotional side of an argument (II. i, 114–40; 162–80). In temporizing with Cassius Brutus falls back on an almost pedantic rhetoric (I. ii, 162–70).

Cæsar utters short precise statements, epigrammatic and oracular in form and consistent with a man accustomed to quick appraisals and decisions, and to his almost divine status. But in his indignation he speaks with concentrated imagery and sustained sentences (III. i, 35–48, 58–73).

Antony's verse has considerable flexibility. The opening lines of his speech to the citizens are frequently end-stopped, and the sentences are short simple statements. Does this suggest hesitancy and caution on Antony's part, or a slow building up of facts expressed simply so as to be easily assimilated? Later, when he has secured the crowd's sympathy he uses longer rhythms (III. ii. 212–32).

Prose is normally used by comic or low characters as befitting their rank, and by contrast with the verse spoken by the courtiers. It can present the stumbling conversation of a Dogberry or Verges, the chop-logic of Feste and Touchstone, the wit and expressiveness of Benedick and Beatrice, the passion of Shylock, and the pensive mood of Hamlet. Shakespeare's concern was always with dramatic effect. Apart from Artemidorus' letter prose occurs in three places in *Julius Cæsar*, in the first scene, in Casca's description of Cæsar's rejection of the crown, and in Brutus' speech to the citizens. The disorderly citizens naturally are given prose speeches. Brutus' unemotional, brilliantly clever speech is cast in prose to emphasize its academic remoteness from its audience (see p. 25). Casca's garrulous, flippant description has a different purpose. It reduces the crown offering episode to a piece of theatrical comedy and at the same time accentuates the tension and suspense Brutus and Cassius are feeling as the important information they are seeking is given with casual indifference to its possible significance. Casca elsewhere speaks in verse, and some editors think that his attitude here is inconsistent with his attitude at the beginning of the scene.

It is sometimes very difficult to understand why Shakespeare changes the dialogue from verse to prose or from one style of blank verse to another. Occasionally the changes may be due to cuts, alterations or additions made to the original play, but in general the variations are deliberately designed to achieve some dramatic effect. They should not, therefore, be overlooked or lightly dismissed in study of the play.

IX

VOCABULARY, IMAGES AND ALLUSIONS

The nature of the vocabulary, images and allusions gives a colouring to the play as a whole, to particular episodes, and to individual characters by direct scene-painting, by emotional modes, and by touching off responses to known associations.

An unusual feature of this play is the significance attached to personal names beyond their face value. Cassius makes the point when he balances the name Cæsar against the name Brutus (I. ii, 142–7); Cinna suffers for it (III. iii); the name Cassius 'honours this corruption' (IV. iii, 15); and Rome held a 'great opinion' of Brutus' name (I. ii, 312–13). The impression given is that of qualities and characteristics, perhaps unrealized in the person concerned, which are associated with him in the mind of the public. Thus the name Cæsar is associated with imperious, absolute rule, and the name Brutus with honour and integrity. Sometimes characters speak their own names out of arrogance or royalty (I. ii, 17, 21), or as public figures (III. ii, 18, 19), or even out of self-pity (IV. ii, 94–5, 107).

Foakes notes the continual interfusing of language and action, 'what is a metaphor, a statement or a hint in the language at one point, is acted out or enters directly into the scene at another'. Particularly is this so in the recurrence of words associated with 'blood' and 'fire' (I. iii, 130; II. i, 168; II. ii, 19–21; III. i, 37; V. iii, 62, etc.). The frequent appearance of 'spirit' in various senses rarefies the emotions and dignifies the tone of the play which might otherwise become crude with its blood letting, violence and strife.

Important threads with their attendant allusions and imagery are the superstitions, portents, omens, dreams and ghost. They reveal Cæsar as a devout man observing religious ceremonies; and by the unnatural symbolic storm in the heavens, and the fulfilment of dreams and prophecies, his stature is enlarged above the ordinary man, and the magnitude of his fall is seen as a destined and universal disaster. Cassius and Brutus, too, finally surrender their beliefs to accept significance of omens and the visitation of the ghost again deepens the sense of inevitable doom.

Complementary in a way to these overtones is the symbolic significance of light and darkness as good and evil. Elsewhere

Shakespeare uses it with deeply moving effect. Here the conspirators are linked with darkness (II. i, 77–85, 277–8) and grope in confusion uncertain where to see sun rise (II. i, 101–11). Brutus wavers between light and dark, his 'state of man' suffering the 'nature of an insurrection'. Uncertain of time in the dark orchard he calls Lucius (light bringer), a character invented by Shakespeare, to light a taper; but he is diverted by Cassius' messages which he reads by the baleful light of the storm. Again Brutus' wish for the harmony of music, also symbolic, is interrupted by the dimming of the taper that heralds Cæsar's ghost (IV. iii, 274). It is possible too that the sickness of Brutus (II. i, 261–4, 268; II. iv, 13–14) and the arrival of the sick Caius Ligarius may symbolize the unhealthy nature of the conspiracy.

Some images are sustained, often with a quibble to display wit or to present an opinion forcefully: I. ii, 294–6, rudeness—sauce—wit—stomach—digest—appetite; I. ii, 302–4, noble—honourable mettle (metal)—wrought—disposed; II. i, 280–7, bond of marriage—excepted—sort—limitation—and possibly, suburbs—harlot. In IV. iii, 218–24 the image here, possibly prompted by the preceding words 'brim-full' and 'height' is extended and applied without forcing: tide—flood—fortune—voyage—bound —shallows—miseries—full sea—afloat—current—ventures. Some shorter linkings of images appear unconscious associations: II. i, 120, fire—kindle—steel; II. i, 144–6, silver—purchase—buy; III. i, 292–4, try … issue (legal). In II. i, 184 Cassius' 'ingrafted' carries on the thought of 'limb—arm' in the previous speech. The well-known image melteth—sweet—spaniel fawning also occurs in III. i, 42–3.

An interesting characteristic of the play is the repetition of phrases and images sometimes apparently accidental at other times significant, as if the speaker is mocking or distorting a former speaker's words. This is true of Antony: III. i, 204–10 with II. i, 174; III. i, 152 with II. i, 180; III. i, 255 and II. i, 166; III. ii, 139 with I. i, 37; V. i, 41–4 with III. i, 43–6; III. ii, 129–34 with II. ii, 88–9. In addition to these there is Antony's disparagement,

III. ii, of the honour Brutus so much prized (I. ii, 86–9; III. ii, 14–15).

X

DEVICES OF STYLE

Elizabethan schooling provided training in rhetoric, that is the art of using words to persuade, to emphasize, and to display eloquence and wit. A most complex system of large numbers of figures of speech, devices of style and processes of thought had been formulated, and Shakespeare made extensive use of them. While for the most part it is enough to be aware that Shakespeare's apparent spontaneous ease in writing discloses a considerable knowledge of rhetoric, the particular use of a few devices in this play should be noted.

Some of the speeches follow the rhetorical patterns prescribed in the text books of the period. The tribute to Brutus (V. v, 68–75) is a 'praise' in that it consists of ordered references to deeds and qualities of person and life. Brutus' speech (II. i, 10–34) is arranged in the manner of a 'theme' with its statement, elaboration, illustration, contradiction, and conclusion. In V. i, 27–49 there is an elaborate 'flyting' based on the adage 'words before blows'. It is, however, in the two speeches in the market place that rhetorical patterns are most obviously used, notably in Brutus' speech. This has been described as the 'most prominent example in Shakespeare of the sustained use of rhetorical schemes'. It has also been described as an example of the Attic style of Roman orators, and again as an example of the Euphistic English style. Each phase of the speech has its own rhetorical pattern, one of which may be illustrated by ll. 23–7: 'As Cæsar . . . ambition' where four statements in the same form are repeated in reverse order with equivalent nouns in place of verbs or adjectives.

Schanzer regards the speech as an 'extremely shrewd and highly effective piece of oratory' uttered in a very difficult situation. Brutus flatters the crowd by inviting them to judge him, to approve his honour, to rank with him as a 'dear friend of Cæsar's', and to accept that love for Rome was his motive. Schanzer continues: 'Then suddenly the question is sprung on them: "Had ... free men?" ... At last an accusation is brought forward, but one of the vaguest and most general sort: Cæsar was ambitious. And at once, before they have time to ask for evidence, there follows the series of rhetorical questions which so ingeniously forestall any objections from his audience. He has brought only the vaguest charge against Cæsar, and yet effectively blocked all further questions from the crowd, shown himself the saviour of his country, and gained the love and admiration of the people.' Granville Barker too, approved: 'I find that it stirs me deeply. I prefer it to Antony's. It wears better. It is very noble prose.'

On the other hand there are those who consider it 'too good for the mob', 'one of the worst speeches ever made by an able and intelligent man', and that its rhetorical structure, and 'its hopelessly abstract subject matter' are the 'utterance of a man whose heart is not in his words. It is a dishonest speech'. In short its failure is marked by the cry from the crowd 'Let him be Cæsar.'

Antony's speech is not so tautly knit nor so intricately patterned as that of Brutus. It makes use of repetition, 'honourable men', and the rhetorical trick of pretending to withhold information while revealing it. It is not so much the form of Antony's words as his skilful infusion of appeals to emotion that stirs the crowd. According to established principles an oration delivered to a crowd to be effective should use appeals to reason, to the feelings, and for confidence in the speaker's integrity. Antony makes use of all three, whereas Brutus appeals mainly to reason and for acceptance of his trustworthiness. Three comments from the crowd on Antony's speech show the appropriate responses:

Methinks there is much reason in his sayings (III. ii, 105)
Poor soul! His eyes are red as fire with weeping (III. ii, 112)
There's not a nobler man in Rome than Antony (III. ii, 113)

The overwhelming effectiveness of the speech springs also from its position as an integral part of the plot and its phrases that echo, sometimes ironically, phrases used previously by the conspirators.

An effort of imagination is required if we are to appreciate the importance and value of the puns that Shakespeare uses so frequently. What has been regarded in recent times as the lowest form of wit, was, as Kellett has shown, used with telling force by Isaiah and St. Paul, and by the Greek dramatists. Among the Elizabethans, who distinguished several different kinds of pun, it was an accepted means of showing intellectual brilliance and verbal dexterity. Shakespeare enlarges its scope: it may produce a simple jest or emphasize a point (Lady Macbeth's

> I'll gild the faces of the grooms withall
> For it must seem their guilt

is horrifyingly emphatic, it is not hysterical). It may sharpen the irony of an aside ('A little more than kin and less than kind'); it may be a flash of bitter insight (in *Romeo and Juliet*, the gay Mercutio mortally wounded says, 'ask for me tomorrow, and you shall find me a grave man'); or it may be employed in an exchange of witticisms.

Sometimes Shakespeare uses the two meanings of a word simultaneously, sometimes the word is repeated bearing a second meaning, or sometimes a word may have the meaning of a word of similar sound imposed on it (in *Love's Labour's Lost* 'haud credo' is confused with 'ow'd grey doe', and in *As You Like It* 'goats' with 'Goths'). There are few puns in this play. 'Basest metal' (I. i, 63) and those forming a link in a sequence of images, 'digest' (I. ii, 295), 'mettle' (I. ii, 303). Those on 'Rome'—'room' (I. ii, 156; III. i, 289) perhaps express bitterness and grimness, as does Antony's cynical 'with a spot I damn him' (IV. i, 6); and that on 'gravity' (II. i, 149) is probably a flash of humour. The puns on 'mend' and 'awl' (I. i, 13-25) while infuriating the tribunes and affording simple amusement for the citizens have an ominous undertone of disorder and revolt.

JULIUS CÆSAR

CHARACTERS

JULIUS CÆSAR
OCTAVIUS CÆSAR } triumvirs after the death
MARK ANTONY } of Julius Cæsar
M. ÆMILIUS LEPIDUS }

CICERO }
PUBLIUS } senators
POPILIUS LENA }

MARCUS BRUTUS }
CASSIUS }
CASCA }
TREBONIUS } conspirators against Julius
LIGARIUS } Cæsar
DECIUS BRUTUS }
METELLUS CIMBER }
CINNA }

FLAVIUS and MARULLUS, tribunes
ARTEMIDORUS, a teacher of rhetoric
A SOOTHSAYER
CINNA, a poet
A POET
LUCILIUS, TITINIUS, MESSALA, YOUNG CATO,
   VOLUMNIUS, friends to Brutus and Cassius
VARRO, CLITUS, CLAUDIUS, STRATO, LUCIUS,
   DARDANIUS, FLAVIUS, LABEO, servants or
   officers to Brutus
PINDARUS, servant to Cassius
CALPHURNIA, wife to Cæsar
PORTIA, wife to Brutus
   Senators Citizens, Guards, Attendants, Soldiers
   SCENE: *At first Rome, then near Sardis and*
                later near Philippi

29

Rome. A street

The citizens may enter first. What are they doing—chattering, shouting, carrying garlands, dancing, flirting, drinking, laughing? Do the tribunes push their way to the front, or meet the crowd from an opposite direction? Another view suggests that the citizens climb from the floor of the theatre, and are driven by the two tribunes 'over the stage'.

1–5   *Hence ... profession.* What effect does this have? Do the citizens scatter, shrink together, become threatening?

1   *idle creatures.* Contemptuous phrase. *idle*, (*a*) unoccupied, (*b*) frivolous.

2   *Is ... holiday.* Indignant and sarcastic.

3   *mechanical*, manual workers, handicraftsmen.

3–5   *you ... profession*, i.e. on working days, if they went into the streets, they would naturally wear the clothes peculiar to their trade. There seems to have been no law, Elizabethan or Roman, on the subject, except that an unemployed Elizabethan was likely to be punished as a rogue under the Statute of 1572.

6   Is the carpenter resentful, respectful, fearful, casual, impudent?

10   *in respect of,* in comparison with. *fine*, highly skilled.

10–11   The cobbler, an incorrigible, garrulous humorist, is unabashed by the threatening authority of the tribunes.

11   *cobbler,* (*a*) clumsy bungler, (*b*) shoe mender.

12   *directly*, plainly.

13–14   *A ... conscience.* The cobbler perhaps has a slighting opinion of trade. See note to l. 24. *use*, practise. *safe conscience*, i.e. (*a*) in spite of his bad workmanship, (*b*) in anticipation of the pun on 'soles'.
    How do the citizens respond to this quibbling?

13–20   Is Marullus being made fun of, is his authority flouted, or is he losing control of the situation?

15   *naughty*, worthless.

17   *out with,* angry with.

18   *out*, out at heels or toes. *yet ... you.* A happy thought! *mend*, (*a*) repair, improve, (*b*) free from sin (a glance back at 'soles'). Does Marullus laugh, turn away enraged, make any gesture?

ACT ONE

SCENE ONE

Enter FLAVIUS, MARULLUS, *and certain* CITIZENS
over the stage

FLAVIUS: Hence! home you idle creatures, get you home.
  Is this a holiday? What, know you not,
  Being mechanical, you ought not walk
  Upon a labouring day without the sign
  Of your profession? Speak, what trade art thou?

FIRST CITIZEN: Why sir, a carpenter.

MARULLUS: Where is thy leather apron and thy rule?
  What dost thou with thy best apparel on?
  You sir, what trade are you?

SECOND CITIZEN: Truly sir, in respect of a fine workman, I
  am but, as you would say, a cobbler.   11

MARULLUS: But what trade art thou? Answer me directly.

SECOND CITIZEN: A trade sir, that I hope I may use with a safe
  conscience; which is indeed sir, a mender of bad soles.

FLAVIUS: What trade thou knave? Thou naughty knave, what
  trade?

SECOND CITIZEN: Nay I beseech you sir, be not out with me;
  yet if you be out sir, I can mend you.

MARULLUS: What meanest thou by that? Mend me, thou saucy
  fellow?   20

SECOND CITIZEN: Why sir, cobble you.

FLAVIUS: Thou art a cobbler, art thou?

23-4 *all . . . awl.* The quibble on 'awl' is emphasized by the clash between 'by' and 'with'. There is an echo perhaps of the proverbial
cobbler sticking to his awl or last.

24 *tradesman's matters.* The cobbler, again emphasizing his dislike of
any connexion with trade, insists that he is above such things as he
is above running after women, and elevates his rank to that of a
surgeon. This may be a topical gibe at the 'gentle (i.e. noble)
craft' of shoemakers highly praised in Dekker's play *The Shoemaker's Holiday*, which was performed in London in 1599. Indeed,
the citizens under the cobbler's leadership are enjoying a kind of
shoemaker's holiday whether they wear out their shoes or not.

25 *with all.* Again the quibble on 'awl' and 'all'.

26 *recover,* (*a*) patch, (*b*) cure. *proper,* fine.

26-7 *As . . . leather,* as fine a fellow as ever wore shoes. Proverbial.

27 *neat's leather,* ox-hide.
  Is Flavius amused, impatient, tolerant?

30 *lead.* How had the cobbler shown his leadership?

31-2 Is this said confidentially, facetiously, as one stating the obvious?

33 *triumph,* entry into Rome in procession of a victorious commander
with the prisoners and booty he has captured.

34-6 *What . . . wheels?* Cæsar was returning from Spain after overthrow-
ing the sons and followers of Pompey, a Roman general. Previously in this civil war Cæsar had defeated Pompey who was
murdered in exile. Cæsar is therefore celebrating a triumph over
his fellow Romans, and is not bringing foreign kings as captives
with their spoil, a circumstance that offended some Romans.

34 *conquest,* i.e. over foreign countries.

35 *tributaries,* conquered rulers who pay money as a price for peace.

36 *in captive bonds,* as prisoners in chains.

41 *chimney-tops.* Anachronisms of this kind are ignored subsequently
in the notes.

48 *replication,* echo.

49 *concave shores,* overhanging banks.

50-3 *And . . . blood?* What does the repetition express—emphasis, irony,
bitterness, sarcasm, contempt, sneering, indignation, a caustic
summary of the citizens' ingratitude?

51 *cull out,* (*a*) pick and choose, (*b*) gather, select choicely (flowers).
A sarcastic word.

53 *blood,* (*a*) slaughter, (*b*) sons. Pompey's elder son had been killed in
battle in Spain.

SECOND CITIZEN: Truly sir, all that I live by is with the awl: I meddle with no tradesman's matters, nor women's matters, but with all. I am indeed sir, a surgeon to old shoes; when they are in great danger, I recover them. As proper men as ever trod upon neat's leather have gone upon my handiwork.

FLAVIUS: But wherefore art not in thy shop today?
Why dost thou lead these men about the streets?   30

SECOND CITIZEN: Truly sir, to wear out their shoes, to get myself into more work. But indeed, sir, we make holiday to see Cæsar, and to rejoice in his triumph.

MARULLUS: Wherefore rejoice? What conquest brings he home?
What tributaries follow him to Rome,
To grace in captive bonds his chariot-wheels?
You blocks, you stones, you worse than senseless things!
O you hard hearts, you cruel men of Rome,
Knew you not Pompey? Many a time and oft
Have you climbed up to walls and battlements,   40
To towers and windows, yea, to chimney-tops,
Your infants in your arms, and there have sat
The livelong day, with patient expectation,
To see great Pompey pass the streets of Rome.
And when you saw his chariot but appear,
Have you not made an universal shout,
That Tiber trembled underneath her banks,
To hear the replication of your sounds
Made in her concave shores?
And do you now put on your best attire?   50
And do you now cull out a holiday?
And do you now strew flowers in his way
That comes in triumph over Pompey's blood?

54-7 *Be . . . ingratitude.* Any movement among the citizens?

56 *intermit*, suspend, put off. *plague*, divine punishment.

59 *sort,* company.

60-2 *weep . . . all*, i.e. their repentance and sorrow should be rendered to the God of the Tiber. What effect is intended by the exaggeration?

63-7 *See . . . ceremonies.* Any gestures or movements?

63 *where,* whether. *basest mettle,* (*a*) brutish feelings, (*b*) basest metal, i.e. lead which is easily melted.

64 *guiltiness,* perhaps suggested by 'basest metal', with a quibble on 'gilt'.
   Are the citizens cowed, pitiful, ashamed or fearful? Accordingly how do they move?

66-7 *Disrobe . . . ceremonies,* strip from the statues of Cæsar any ceremonial adornments you may find.

69 *feast of Lupercal.* An annual festival of purification and fertility in honour of the god Lupercus. Shakespeare combines two historically distinct events, Cæsar's triumph and the feast of the Lupercalia for dramatic reasons that become apparent in the next scene (see Appendix I p. 208).

71 *trophies,* decorations in honour of Cæsar.

72 *the vulgar,* the common people.

74 *growing feathers,* increasing support. *wing,* power, authority.

75 *pitch,* height. 'Pitch' was often used of the height to which a falcon soared before it swooped on its prey, a meaning developed in the next line.

76-7 *Who . . . fearfulness,* i.e. Cæsar would, like a falcon, rise beyond the reach of ordinary folk and keep all of us in slavish fear lest he should strike.
   This scene has been described as an imaginative kind of prologue foreshadowing the main action of the play. The ease with which the crowd is swayed by oratory when a dead hero is praised, the popularity of Cæsar with the common people, the hostility of some Romans towards Cæsar, the threat of disaster following wrong doing, and, to Elizabethan ears, ominous echoes of rebellion in the cobbler's quibbling on 'mend' and 'awl' are themes developed later.

Be gone!
Run to your houses, fall upon your knees,
Pray to the gods to intermit the plague
That needs must light on this ingratitude.
FLAVIUS: Go, go, good countrymen, and for this fault,
Assemble all the poor men of your sort;
Draw them to Tiber banks, and weep your tears   60
Into the channel, till the lowest stream
Do kiss the most exalted shores of all.   [*Exeunt all the Citizens*
See, where their basest mettle be not moved;
They vanish tongue-tied in their guiltiness.
Go you down that way towards the Capitol;
This way will I. Disrobe the images,
If you do find them decked with ceremonies.
MARULLUS: May we do so?
You know it is the feast of Lupercal.
FLAVIUS: It is no matter; let no images   70
Be hung with Caesar's trophies. I'll about,
And drive away the vulgar from the streets;
So do you too, where you perceive them thick.
These growing feathers plucked from Cæsar's wing
Will make him fly an ordinary pitch,
Who else would soar above the view of men,
And keep us all in servile fearfulness.   [*Exeunt*

Rome. A street

An entry in ceremonial procession heralded probably by a flourish of trumpets and accompanied by other music. Is Cæsar on foot or carried in a chair or litter or under a canopy? Where is the crown?

S.D. Antony . . . course, i.e. stripped for running.

Shakespeare compresses Cæsar's triumph, the feast of the Lupercalia and the assassination into two days instead of the actual time of some six months. The combining of the first two is dramatically an economical way of showing Cæsar's power and relationships with the people. By placing the ceremony on the eve of Cæsar's visit to the Capitol to be formally offered the crown, Shakespeare has linked it with the Elizabethan coronation ceremony of the recognition and procession which took place on the day before the actual crowning (see Introduction p. 10).

1–11   Some have seen in Cæsar's first appearance and speeches a caricature of greatness, a superstition-ridden, credulous old man half-ashamed of believing an old-wives' tale. On the other hand he is addressed in a way which implies his greatness and majesty, and not that he is ridiculous or senile. In Elizabethan eyes, as a prospective ruler he might naturally be concerned about obtaining an heir (see Introduction p. 10).

    Is he brutal in proclaiming Calphurnia's failing in public, humanely trying to help her or anxious to secure the succession should he become king?

1   *Peace . . . speaks.* Any gesture and movement?

2   *Here, my lord.* Any movement and gesture of obedience?

4   *his course.* At the feast of the Lupercalia the priests ('young men' according to Plutarch), stripped to a girdle, ran through the city striking with leather thongs any woman who presented herself in the way. It was believed that such a blow would cure barren women of their childlessness.

7   *for . . . say.* Is Cæsar covering up his own belief in superstition, or that of Calphurnia (see II. ii, 13 ff). Is he revering the wisdom of the elders or being pious?

9   *curse*, i.e. affliction from the gods which might well be removed by the 'holy' ceremony.

12   What pitch, speed, intonation make the soothsayer's cry effective?

15   *press*, crowd.

17   *Cæsar . . . hear.* Is Cæsar pompous and arrogant in using the third person, or is it a natural way of addressing a man hidden in the throng? See also l. 212.

SCENE TWO

Flourish. Enter CÆSAR, ANTONY *for the course,* CALPHURNIA, PORTIA, DECIUS, CICERO, BRUTUS, CASSIUS, CASCA, *a* SOOTHSAYER, *a great crowd following, after them* FLAVIUS *and* MARULLUS

CÆSAR: Calphurnia.
CASCA:　　　　　　　Peace ho! Cæsar speaks.
CÆSAR:　　　　　　　　　　　　Calphurnia.
CALPHURNIA: Here my lord.
CÆSAR: Stand you directly in Antonius' way,
　　When he doth run his course. Antonius.
ANTONY: Cæsar, my lord?
CÆSAR: Forget not, in your speed, Antonius,
　　To touch Calphurnia; for our elders say,
　　The barren, touched in this holy chase,
　　Shake off their sterile curse.
ANTONY:　　　　　　　I shall remember.
　　When Cæsar says, 'Do this', it is performed.　　　　10
CÆSAR: Set on, and leave no ceremony out.　　　[*Music*
SOOTHSAYER: Cæsar!
CÆSAR: Ha! Who calls?
CASCA: Bid every noise be still. Peace yet again!
CÆSAR: Who is it in the press that calls on me?
　　I hear a tongue shriller than all the music
　　Cry 'Cæsar!' Speak; Cæsar is turned to hear.

37

18   *ides of March,* 15 March.

19   *A ... March.* Possibly repeated because of Cæsar's deafness. It is
      ironical that the warning should be given to Cæsar by Brutus.

24   *He ... pass.* An ominous and tense moment as Cæsar and the
      soothsayer face each other.
             Cæsar sees that he is not an informer or mischief maker. Is
      he superstitious? How does he dismiss the soothsayer—contemptu-
      ously, gently, confidently, laughingly, brusquely, with relief?

S.D. *Sennet,* a flourish of trumpets.

25   *order ... course,* the state of the racing.

26–30 Is Brutus aloof, preoccupied, curt, unfriendly, impatient, sarcastic,
      cold, sardonic, moody, tired?

28   *gamesome,* sportive, fond of games and merrymaking.

29   *quick spirit,* lively nature, speed.

30   *Let ... desires.* Is this a suggestion that Cassius too is 'gamesome'?

34   *wont,* accustomed.

35–6 *You ... you,* you have put a curb upon our friendship and have
      treated my love with aloofness.

35   *bear ... hand,* ride like a horse too hard upon the curb. *strange,*
      distant, estranged.

37–9 *veiled ... myself,* my looks have been clouded over, they have been
      directed entirely on myself.

39–40 *Vexed ... difference,* I have lately been troubled with conflicting
      feelings.

41   *Conceptions ... myself,* thoughts solely concerning myself.

42   *give some soil,* blacken somewhat.

45   *Nor ... neglect,* nor read into my neglect of them anything more.
             What dramatic values has this reconciliation? Does it show
      Brutus divided in mind the readier to accept Cassius' suggestions,
      does his feeling of owing love and friendship to Cassius make him
      more vulnerable, does it prepare for the quarrel and reconciliation
      in IV. iii?

Act One, Scene Two

SOOTHSAYER: Beware the ides of March.

CÆSAR: What man is that?

BRUTUS: A soothsayer bids you beware the ides of March.

CÆSAR: Set him before me, let me see his face.   20

CASSIUS: Fellow, come from the throng, look upon Cæsar.

CÆSAR: What say'st thou to me now? Speak once again.

SOOTHSAYER: Beware the ides of March.

CÆSAR: He is a dreamer, let us leave him. Pass.

> [*Sennet. Exeunt all except Brutus and Cassius*

CASSIUS: Will you go see the order of the course?

BRUTUS: Not I.

CASSIUS: I pray you do.

BRUTUS: I am not gamesome; I do lack some part
Of that quick spirit that is in Antony.
Let me not hinder, Cassius, your desires;   30
I'll leave you.

CASSIUS: Brutus, I do observe you now of late;
I have not from your eyes that gentleness
And show of love as I was wont to have.
You bear too stubborn and too strange a hand
Over your friend that loves you.

BRUTUS: Cassius,
Be not deceived. If I have veiled my look,
I turn the trouble of my countenance
Merely upon myself. Vexed I am
Of late with passions of some difference,   40
Conceptions only proper to myself,
Which give some soil perhaps to my behaviours.
But let not therefore my good friends be grieved—
Among which number, Cassius, be you one—
Nor construe any further my neglect,
Than that poor Brutus with himself at war,
Forgets the shows of love to other men.

CASSIUS: Then Brutus, I have much mistook your passion;

49   *By means whereof*, for that reason. *buried*, kept to itself.

54   *'Tis just*, exactly, that is true.

56   *turn*, reflect.

58   *shadow*, reflection, picture.
59–90 Cassius skilfully takes Brutus' words ll. 36–8 and turns them to his
       own account, ll. 51, 56–8, 67–70.
59   *best respect*, highest reputation.
60   *Except immortal Cæsar*. Is this ironical, the deft thin edge of a wedge
       in detaching Cæsar from the others in Brutus' mind, an attempt to
       associate Cæsar with the 'age's yoke'?
62   *had his eyes*, realized his position, saw how he stood.

66   *Therefore*, as for that. Alternatively Cassius may ignore Brutus'
       question.

69   *modestly*, without exaggeration.

71   *jealous on*, suspicious of. *gentle*, noble.
72   *laughter*, laughing stock. Some editors prefer the emendation
       'laugher'.
73   *ordinary*, (*a*) common, (*b*) tavern (Arden).
74   *To . . . protester*, to cheapen my love by supporting it with com-
       monplace oaths to every newcomer who declares his love for me.
76   *after scandal*, afterwards abuse, tell lies about.
77–8   *profess . . . rout*, claim friendship with all and sundry when mellow
       at a banquet.
79–80 *What . . . king*. Does Brutus show alarm, concern, surprise? *I
       . . . king*. Brutus involuntarily speaks his thought. Which word or
       words should be emphasized?
80   *Ay . . . it*. What feelings should Cassius display—surprise, satisfac-
       tion, amusement, pleasure?

By means whereof this breast of mine hath buried
Thoughts of great value, worthy cogitations.　　　　　50
Tell me good Brutus, can you see your face?
BRUTUS: No Cassius; for the eye sees not itself
But by reflection, by some other things.
CASSIUS: 'Tis just;
And it is very much lamented Brutus,
That you have no such mirrors as will turn
Your hidden worthiness into your eye,
That you might see your shadow. I have heard,
Where many of the best respect in Rome—
Except immortal Cæsar—speaking of Brutus,　　　　　60
And groaning underneath this age's yoke,
Have wished that noble Brutus had his eyes.
BRUTUS: Into what dangers would you lead me Cassius,
That you would have me seek into myself
For that which is not in me?
CASSIUS: Therefore good Brutus, be prepared to hear;
And since you know you cannot see yourself
So well as by reflection, I your glass,
Will modestly discover to yourself
That of yourself which you yet know not of.　　　　　70
And be not jealous on me, gentle Brutus.
Were I a common laughter, or did use
To stale with ordinary oaths my love
To every new protester; if you know
That I do fawn on men, and hug them hard,
And after scandal them; or if you know
That I profess myself in banqueting
To all the rout, then hold me dangerous. [Flourish, and shout.
BRUTUS: What means this shouting? I do fear the people
Choose Cæsar for their king.
CASSIUS:　　　　　　　　Ay, do you fear it?　　　　　80
Then must I think you would not have it so.

41

83   *But . . . long?* Brutus changes the subject—why? Is he impatient, innocent of any idea of conspiracy, attentive to Cassius?

85   *general good*, good of all in general.

86   *Set . . . other*, even though honour on the one hand implies death from another point of view, I will make no difference between them.

88   *speed*, prosper, give success. *as*, in that.

91   *outward favour*, features, facial expression.

92   *honour . . . story*. Cassius again picks up a word from Brutus and uses it as a link.

94   *my single self*, speaking for myself.

95   *as lief not be*, rather die. *as lief . . . to be*. A quibbling, bitter repetition of sounds.

96   *such . . . myself*, i.e. Cæsar, who is a mere man like Cassius.

101   *chafing with*, beating upon.

105   *Accoutred*, in armour.

109   *stemming . . . controversy*, breasting it in rivalry.

112–   *as . . . bear*. The Roman poet Virgil, writing after Cæsar's death,
  14   told a story of the founding of Rome by Æneas, a refugee from Troy. Æneas carried his father Anchises on his back from the burning city (*Æneid*, II. 721).

       What values have this simile—the addition of Roman colour, by recalling the tradition of Rome to appeal to Brutus, to insinuate that Cæsar is now senile, to show Cassius' arrogance in likening himself to the ancestor of Julius Cæsar?

115   *man*. Contemptuous.

BRUTUS: I would not Cassius, yet I love him well.
But wherefore do you hold me here so long?
What is it that you would impart to me?
If it be aught toward the general good,
Set honour in one eye and death i' th' other,
And I will look on both indifferently;
For let the gods so speed me as I love
The name of honour more than I fear death.

CASSIUS: I know that virtue to be in you Brutus,   90
As well as I do know your outward favour.
Well, honour is the subject of my story.
I cannot tell what you and other men
Think of this life; but for my single self,
I had as lief not be, as live to be
In awe of such a thing as I myself.
I was born free as Cæsar, so were you;
We both have fed as well, and we can both
Endure the winter's cold as well as he.
For once, upon a raw and gusty day,   100
The troubled Tiber chafing with her shores,
Cæsar said to me, 'Darest thou Cassius now
Leap in with me into this angry flood,
And swim to yonder point?' Upon the word,
Accoutred as I was, I plunged in,
And bade him follow; so indeed he did.
The torrent roared, and we did buffet it
With lusty sinews, throwing it aside,
And stemming it with hearts of controversy.
But ere we could arrive the point proposed,   110
Cæsar cried, 'Help me Cassius, or I sink.'
I, as Æneas, our great ancestor,
Did from the flames of Troy upon his shoulder
The old Anchises bear, so from the waves of Tiber
Did I the tired Cæsar. And this man

43

116   *Is . . . god*, i.e. in the worship given him by the people and by the authority he is assuming.

117   *creature*, slave.

119   *He . . . Spain*. Any gesture to accompany this new train of thought?

122   *His . . . fly*, (*a*) the colour drained from his lips as a coward soldier deserted his colours, (*b*) his lips turned pale with fear.
     Is Cassius' demonstration of Cæsar's cowardice just?

123   *bend*, glance.

124   *his*, its.

126   *write . . . books*, i.e. his oratory was so eloquent that Romans wrote down his speeches. *books*, tablets.

127   *Give . . . Titinius*. Cassius mimics Cæsar's accents.

128   *amaze*, astound.

129   *temper*, constitution, nature.

130   *get . . . alone*, should outstrip all in this majestic Roman world and win the supreme honour.

135 ff   *Why. . . .* Does Cassius ignore Brutus' comment deliberately, or because he is so roused?

135   *man*. Is this a sign of impatience or familiarity?

136   *Colossus*. The Colossus of Rhodes, one of the seven wonders of the world, was a gigantic statue of Apollo. It was believed, erroneously, that its legs bestrode the entrance of the harbour.
     The bursts of applause intensify the effect of Cassius' speeches on Brutus. Dramatically the ironic contrast between Cassius' enmity towards Cæsar and Cæsar's popularity with the citizens shown side by side is most effective.

138   *dishonourable*, unhonoured because under Cæsar they are slaves, and therefore no statues would be erected in their honour.

140   *in our stars*. It was believed that the positions of the planets and stars in the zodiac at the time of a man's birth determined his character and his fortunes.

142   *Brutus and Cæsar*. Dextrously Cassius now involves Brutus directly.

143   *be sounded more*, be more celebrated.

144   *fair*, i.e. in written appearance.

145   *sound*, pronounce. *it . . . well*, it sounds as pleasantly in the mouth.

146   *Weigh*, (*a*) weigh, (*b*) consider carefully, i.e. weigh one's words, *heavy*, (*a*) important, (*b*) heavy in weight. *conjure*, use the power of the names to raise up spirits.

Is now become a god, and Cassius is
A wretched creature, and must bend his body,
If Cæsar carelessly but nod on him.
He had a fever when he was in Spain,
And when the fit was on him, I did mark   120
How he did shake. 'Tis true, this god did shake;
His coward lips did from their colour fly,
And that same eye whose bend doth awe the world
Did lose his lustre; I did hear him groan;
Ay, and that tongue of his, that bade the Romans
Mark him and write his speeches in their books,
Alas, it cried, 'Give me some drink Titinius,'
As a sick girl. Ye gods, it doth amaze me
A man of such a feeble temper should
So get the start of the majestic world,   130
And bear the palm alone.   *[Shout. Flourish*
BRUTUS: Another general shout?
    I do believe that these applauses are
    For some new honours that are heaped on Cæsar.
CASSIUS: Why man, he doth bestride the narrow world
    Like a Colossus, and we petty men
    Walk under his huge legs, and peep about
    To find ourselves dishonourable graves.
    Men at some time are masters of their fates:
    The fault, dear Brutus, is not in our stars,   140
    But in ourselves, that we are underlings.
    Brutus and Cæsar. What should be in that 'Cæsar'?
    Why should that name be sounded more than yours?
    Write them together, yours is as fair a name;
    Sound them, it doth become the mouth as well;
    Weigh them, it is as heavy; conjure with 'em,
    Brutus will start a spirit as soon as Cæsar.
    Now in the names of all the gods at once,
    Upon what meat doth this our Cæsar feed,

45

151   *bloods*, men of courage and spirit.

152   *the great flood*. In classical myths Zeus destroyed mankind by a
      flood. He preserved, however, Deucalion and his wife Pyrrha
      who, on the advice of an oracle, repopulated the world by throw-
      behind them stones which turned into men and women.

153, *one man . . . one only man*. Bitter impassioned emphasis. *one man*,
5, 7 i.e. one famous man.

155   *walks*. Some editors prefer Rowe's emendation 'walls'.

156   *Rome . . . room*. What does the pun express—contempt, bitter-
      ness, sarcasm, mirth?

156-7 *Now . . . man*, it is rightly called Rome (room), since there is room
      in it for only one real man.

158- *O . . . king*. This is the climax to which Cassius has been working.
61   Its appeal to Brutus is couched in references to tradition, the great-
      ness of the past, and the hatred of kings. Which words need
      emphasis to carry Cassius' insinuation?

159   *a Brutus once*. Lucius Junius Brutus who helped to drive out of
      Rome the royal Tarquin family and to establish a republic.
      Brutus claimed descent from him. *brooked*, tolerated endured.

160   *eternal*, utter, absolute. An emphatic word. *to . . . state*, to reign, to
      hold his court.

162 ff Is Brutus agitated, calm, controlled, uncertain, cold, irritated,
      cautious? Do the short sentences suggest that he is stirred or do they
      form an orderly balanced pattern?

162   *nothing jealous*, not in the least doubtful. Brutus echoes Cassius'
      plea, l. 71.

163   *aim*, guess.

165 ff Is Brutus' postponement due to indecision, the wish to avoid
      Cassius' pressure, divided loyalty?

171   *chew*, think. This was not formerly a slang expression.

172   *villager*, a labourer in a village.

172-5 *Brutus . . . us*. A statement uttered with energy and conviction.

173   *son*, citizen.

176   *weak words*. Is Cassius fulsome, flattering, humble, genuine, dis-
      appointed, ironic?

176-7 *struck . . . fire*, i.e. as from a flint.
      What position on the stage should Brutus and Cassius have so
      that they can comment on the entry of Cæsar?

180   *sour*, dry, sarcastic.

181   *worthy*, worthy of.

That he is grown so great? Age, thou art shamed.   150
Rome, thou hast lost the breed of noble bloods.
When went there by an age since the great flood,
But it was famed with more than with one man?
When could they say, till now, that talked of Rome,
That her wide walks encompassed but one man?
Now is it Rome indeed, and room enough,
When there is in it but one only man.
O you and I have heard our fathers say,
There was a Brutus once that would have brooked
Th' eternal devil to keep his state in Rome   160
As easily as a king.

BRUTUS: That you do love me, I am nothing jealous;
What you would work me to, I have some aim:
How I have thought of this, and of these times,
I shall recount hereafter. For this present,
I would not, so with love I might entreat you,
Be any further moved. What you have said,
I will consider; what you have to say,
I will with patience hear, and find a time
Both meet to hear and answer such high things.   170
Till then, my noble friend, chew upon this:
Brutus had rather be a villager
Than to repute himself a son of Rome
Under these hard conditions as this time
Is like to lay upon us.

CASSIUS: I am glad
That my weak words have struck but thus much show
Of fire from Brutus.

BRUTUS: The games are done, and Cæsar is returning.

CASSIUS: As they pass by, pluck Casca by the sleeve,
And he will, after his sour fashion, tell you   180
What hath proceeded worthy note today.

47

s.d. *Train*, followers in procession.

182–8 *But ... senators*. Perhaps uttered rapidly and with surprise since apparently honours and applause had been given to Cæsar.

   What movements or bearing justify Brutus' descriptions?

184 *chidden*, cowed, scolded.

185 *Cicero*. The famous Roman orator.

186 *ferret*, red with a suggestion of spiteful anger. The ferret, an albino, has red eyes and is bad tempered.

188 *crossed in conference*, opposed in discussion.

189 *Casca ... is*. Any movement?

192–3 *Let ... a-nights*, Cæsar consoles himself with the society of Antony who is not lean and hungry.

197 *given*, disposed.

198 *Would ... fatter*. Is this serious or in jest?

199 *Yet ... fear*, i.e. as Cæsar, the public figure, he must maintain an appearance of fearlessness. *my name*. Is this pride, conceit, boasting, simple truth?

203–4 *He ... Antony*. Antony has a reputation as a 'masker and a reveller' (see V. i, 62).

202–3 *he ... men*, he sees the motives behind men's deeds.

204 *he ... music*, i.e. according to the Elizabethans such lack of harmony indicated a treacherous mind. Contrast Brutus' interest in music (IV. iii, 257–9).

205 *sort*, way.

206 *As ... himself*, wryly, sardonically.

   Is this character sketch of Cassius to suggest to the audience how much trust they can put in Cassius' description of Cæsar, or to demonstrate Cæsar's ability to judge men?

213 *deaf*. Why did Shakespeare add this—to show Cæsar as infirm and ailing, to symbolize his disregard of sinister (left hand) omens, to liken Cæsar to Elizabeth?

   What words apply to Cæsar—mocked, childish, belittled, senile, self-dramatizing, boastful, sincere, shrewd, obtuse, superstitious, simple, self-deceiving, courageous, unintelligent?

Enter CÆSAR *and his Train*

BRUTUS: I will do so. But look you Cassius,
   The angry spot doth glow on Cæsar's brow,
   And all the rest look like a chidden train:
   Calphurnia's cheek is pale, and Cicero
   Looks with such ferret and such fiery eyes
   As we have seen him in the Capitol,
   Being crossed in conference by some senators.
CASSIUS: Casca will tell us what the matter is.
CÆSAR: Antonius.   190
ANTONY: Cæsar?
CÆSAR: Let me have men about me that are fat,
   Sleek-headed men, and such as sleep a-nights.
   Yond Cassius has a lean and hungry look;
   He thinks too much. Such men are dangerous.
ANTONY: Fear him not Cæsar, he's not dangerous.
   He is a noble Roman, and well given.
CÆSAR: Would he were fatter. But I fear him not.
   Yet if my name were liable to fear,
   I do not know the man I should avoid   200
   So soon as that spare Cassius. He reads much,
   He is a great observer, and he looks
   Quite through the deeds of men. He loves no plays,
   As thou dost Antony; he hears no music;
   Seldom he smiles, and smiles in such a sort
   As if he mocked himself, and scorned his spirit
   That could be moved to smile at any thing.
   Such men as he be never at heart's ease
   Whiles they behold a greater than themselves,
   And therefore are they very dangerous.   210
   I rather tell thee what is to be feared
   Than what I fear; for always I am Cæsar.
   Come on my right hand, for this ear is deaf,

217   *sad*, serious.
      Why should Casca speak in prose? Elsewhere he speaks in verse.
219 ff Is Casca reluctant, too bored, too fatigued to tell?

221–3 *Why . . . a-shouting*. Is this summary spoken casually, scornfully
       with indifference, cynically, with a drawl, as of no importance?
       Casca has very important information which Brutus and
       Cassius are desperately anxious to know. He exasperates them by
       withholding the full story until their urgent, insistent questioning
       assures him of an audience.

229–30 *and . . . other*. Any gesture?
230–1   *mine honest neighbours*. Casca sarcastically mimics a colloquial,
        phrase.

236   *mere foolery*, ridiculous performance.

239   *fain*, gladly.

242   *still*, always.

244   *chopped*, chapped, cracked with work and cold.
245–6 *stinking . . . swounded*. See Introduction p. 11.

And tell me truly what thou think'st of him.

[*Sennet. Exeunt Cæsar and his Train*

CASCA: You pulled me by the cloak; would you speak with me?

BRUTUS: Ay Casca, tell us what hath chanced today
That Cæsar looks so sad.

CASCA: Why you were with him, were you not?

BRUTUS: I should not then ask Casca what had chanced. 220

CASCA: Why there was a crown offered him; and being offered him, he put it by with the back of his hand, thus; and then the people fell a-shouting.

BRUTUS: What was the second noise for?

CASCA: Why for that too.

CASSIUS: They shouted thrice. What was the last cry for?

CASCA: Why for that too.

BRUTUS: Was the crown offered him thrice? 228

CASCA: Ay marry was't, and he put it by thrice, every time gentler than other; and at every putting-by mine honest neighbours shouted.

CASSIUS: Who offered him the crown?

CASCA: Why Antony.

BRUTUS: Tell us the manner of it, gentle Casca. 234

CASCA: I can as well be hanged as tell the manner of it. It was mere foolery; I did not mark it. I saw Mark Antony offer him a crown, yet 'twas not a crown neither, 'twas one of these coronets; and as I told you, he put it by once: but for all that, to my thinking, he would fain have had it. Then he offered it to him again; then he put it by again; but to my thinking, he was very loath to lay his fingers off it. And then he offered it the third time; he put it the third time by; and still as he refused it, the rabblement hooted, and clapped their chopped hands, and threw up their sweaty night-caps, and uttered such a deal of stinking breath because Cæsar refused the crown, that it had almost choked Cæsar; for he swounded, and

247   *I . . . laugh.* What aroused his mirth—contempt for Cæsar, the silliness of the citizens?

249   *But . . . swound?* Is this a jeering question or to confirm his opinion of Cæsar?

250-1   *He . . . speechless.* Any mimicking?

252   *'Tis . . . falling sickness.* Most editors insert a heavy stop after 'like and interpret, 'That is quite likely: he is an epileptic'. The Folio text, however, with no punctuation after 'like' makes good sense, 'It really sounds as if he has epilepsy' (Sisson).

254   *falling sickness,* i.e. under the increasing power of Cæsar their standing is being lowered.

257-8   *as . . . theatre.* Is Casca hinting that the whole business was carefully staged before the citizens?

261-2   *plucked . . . cut,* i.e. to assure the citizens of his honesty of purpose.

262   *An,* if.

263   *man . . . occupation,* man of my hands.

266   *their worships.* Cæsar's courtesy or Casca's sarcasm?

267   *infirmity,* weakness.

268   *Alas good soul.* More mimicry.

276-7   *Nay . . . again,* i.e. you surely do not expect me to understand gibberish. Cæsar puns on 'Greek' in l. 274 as well as in l. 278.

278-9   *it . . . me,* it was double Dutch to me.

279-   *Marullus . . . silence.* How is this received—any movements,
80   gestures or stillness?

280   *scarfs,* adornments.

fell down at it. And for mine own part, I durst not laugh, for fear of opening my lips and receiving the bad air.

CASSIUS: But soft I pray you; what, did Cæsar swound? 249

CASCA: He fell down in the market-place, and foamed at mouth, and was speechless.

BRUTUS: 'Tis very like he hath the falling sickness.

CASSIUS: No, Cæsar hath it not; but you, and I, And honest Casca, we have the falling sickness.

CASCA: I know not what you mean by that, but I am sure Cæsar fell down. If the tag-rag people did not clap him and hiss him, according as he pleased and displeased them, as they use to do the players in the theatre, I am no true man.

BRUTUS: What said he when he came unto himself? 259

CASCA: Marry, before he fell down, when he perceived the common herd was glad he refused the crown, he plucked me ope his doublet, and offered them his throat to cut. An I had been a man of any occupation, if I would not have taken him at a word, I would I might go to hell among the rogues. And so he fell. When he came to himself again, he said, if he had done or said anything amiss, he desired their worships to think it was his infirmity. Three or four wenches where I stood cried, 'Alas good soul,' and forgave him with all their hearts. But there's no heed to be taken of them; if Cæsar had stabbed their mothers, they would have done no less. 270

BRUTUS: And after that, he came thus sad away?

CASCA: Ay.

CASSIUS: Did Cicero say any thing?

CASCA: Ay, he spoke Greek.

CASSIUS: To what effect?

CASCA: Nay, an I tell you that, I'll ne'er look you i' th' face again. But those that understood him smiled at one another. and shook their heads; but for mine own part, it was Greek to me. I could tell you more news too: Marullus and Flavius, for pulling scarfs off Cæsar's images, are put to silence. Fare you

290   *quick mettle*, lively, spirited, keen—by contrast with 'blunt'.

293   *However*, although. *tardy form*, sluggish mannerism, or drawling speech.

294   *rudeness*, bluntness. *wit*, intelligence.

295   *stomach*, desire, inclination.

301   *the world*, i .e. the Roman world, or the state of affairs in Rome.

303–4   *honourable . . . disposed*. Another quibble on 'metal' sustained through 'noble', 'mettle', 'wrought'.

303   *wrought*, worked (as a metal).

304   *disposed*, inclined by nature.

307   *bear me hard*, has a grudge against me.

308–9   *If . . . me*. Editors are divided in their interpretation of this: (*a*) If I were Brutus, and Brutus were Cassius he would not sway me, (*b*) If I were Brutus and Cæsar were Cassius, Cæsar would not sway me.

       The first interpretation implies villainy and cynicism in Cassius, the second refers to a passage in Plutarch in which Brutus is warned against Cæsar's blandishments.

310   *several hands*, different handwriting.

314   *ambition*. The word had evil associations: overmastering desire for honours, selfish unscrupulous pursuit of power. *glanced*, hinted.

well. There was more foolery yet, if I could remember it.   281

CASSIUS: Will you sup with me tonight, Casca?

CASCA: No, I am promised forth.

CASSIUS: Will you dine with me tomorrow?

CASCA: Ay, if I be alive, and your mind hold, and your dinner
worth the eating.

CASSIUS: Good; I will expect you.

CASCA: Do so. Farewell both.   [*Exit*

BRUTUS: What a blunt fellow is this grown to be!
He was quick mettle when he went to school.   290

CASSIUS: So is he now in execution
Of any bold or noble enterprise,
However he puts on this tardy form.
This rudeness is a sauce to his good wit,
Which gives men stomach to digest his words
With better appetite.

BRUTUS: And so it is. For this time I will leave you.
Tomorrow, if you please to speak with me,
I will come home to you; or, if you will,
Come home to me, and I will wait for you.   300

CASSIUS: I will do so. Till then, think of the world. [*Exit Brutus*
Well Brutus, thou art noble; yet I see
Thy honourable mettle may be wrought
From that it is disposed. Therefore it is meet
That noble minds keep ever with their likes;
For who so firm that cannot be seduced?
Cæsar doth bear me hard, but he loves Brutus.
If I were Brutus now, and he were Cassius,
He should not humour me. I will this night,
In several hands, in at his windows throw,   310
As if they came from several citizens,
Writings, all tending to the great opinion
That Rome holds of his name; wherein obscurely
Cæsar's ambition shall be glanced at.

315   *him*, himself.

316   *or . . . endure*, or else suffer worse under Cæsar's rule.

In a soliloquy characters normally tell the truth. What words apply to Cassius—honourable, opportunist, cynical, malicious, unscrupulous, patriotic, vengeful, treacherous, envious, Vice-like?

Rome. A street

The sudden rattling thunder adds dramatic point to Cassius' concluding couplet.

Disorder in the heavens was believed to correspond with disorder in kingdoms and with threats to rulers of states. Here the storm pervading the whole scene symbolizes the impending disasters in Rome.

How do Cicero and Casca meet? Is Casca running, searching, warily moving? Is he staring to identify Cicero, with fright, or at the sky?

3   *moved*, disturbed, frightened. *sway of earth*, ordained order, realm of earth (Arden).

4   *Shakes . . . unfirm.* An echo of Cassius' threat to 'shake' Cæsar with perhaps a glance at Cæsar's 'infirmity'.

6   *rived*, split.

7   *ambitious ocean*, the ocean thrusting itself up, the mounting seas.

10   *dropping fire*, thunderbolts, electrical discharges.

11   *civil . . . heaven*, war among the gods.

12   *saucy*, insolent.

Why does Casca now speak in verse? Is it appropriate to his description, to his mood, or is his character inconsistent?

14   *Why . . . wonderful?* What is Cicero's attitude—fearless, rapturous, rational, sceptical, calm?

18   *Not sensible of*, insensitive to, not feeling.

21   *glazed*, stared, glared. *surly*, haughty air, imperious mien.

22   *annoying*, injuring.

22-3   *drawn . . . heap*, huddled together.

23   *ghastly*, (*a*) terrified, (*b*) ghost like.

24   *Transformed*, beside themselves.

And after this let Cæsar seat him sure,
For we will shake him, or worse days endure.   [*Exit*

SCENE THREE

Thunder and lightning. Enter CASCA *and* CICERO

CICERO: Good even, Casca: brought you Cæsar home?
  Why are you breathless, and why stare you so?
CASCA: Are not you moved, when all the sway of earth
  Shakes like a thing unfirm? O Cicero,
  I have seen tempests, when the scolding winds
  Have rived the knotty oaks, and I have seen
  Th' ambitious ocean swell, and rage, and foam,
  To be exalted with the threat'ning clouds;
  But never till tonight, never till now,
  Did I go through a tempest dropping fire.   10
  Either there is a civil strife in heaven,
  Or else the world, too saucy with the gods,
  Incenses them to send destruction.
CICERO: Why, saw you any thing more wonderful?
CASCA: A common slave—you know him well by sight—
  Held up his left hand, which did flame and burn
  Like twenty torches joined; and yet his hand,
  Not sensible of fire, remained unscorched.
  Besides—I ha' not since put up my sword—
  Against the Capitol I met a lion,   20
  Who glazed upon me, and went surly by,
  Without annoying me. And there were drawn
  Upon a heap, a hundred ghastly women,
  Transformed with their fear, who swore they saw
  Men, all in fire, walk up and down the streets.

26 *bird of night*, owl.

28 *prodigies*, unnatural events.

29 *conjointly meet*, coincide, happen together.

30 *These . . . natural*, this is the explanation of them, they are only natural events.

31 *portentous*, ominous, ill-omened.

32 *climate*, country, region. Astrologically it is that part of the earth controlled by a planet.

    Is Casca excited, superstitious, gesticulating, impassioned, fearful, credulous, stupefied, hysterical, shocked?

33 *strange-disposed time*, unusual course of events.

34–5 *construe . . . themselves*, interpret things according to their own view, and quite contrary to their real significance. An anticipation of ll. 62 ff.

43 *A . . . men*. Cassius takes the omens as favourable to his plans and hostile to Cæsar (see ll. 70–8).

48 *unbraced*, with doublet untied.

49 *thunderstone*, thunderbolt.

50 *cross*, forked.

52 *in the aim*, directly in its path.

    What is Cassius' attitude to the storm—fearful, terrified, indifferent, challenging, rejoicing, exhilarated, justified, overwrought, hysterical?

53 *tempt the heavens*, challenge the gods.

And yesterday the bird of night did sit,
Even at noon-day, upon the market-place,
Hooting and shrieking. When these prodigies
Do so conjointly meet, let not men say,
'These are their reasons—they are natural'.   30
For I believe, they are portentous things
Unto the climate that they point upon.
CICERO: Indeed, it is a strange-disposed time.
But men may construe things after their fashion,
Clean from the purpose of the things themselves.
Comes Cæsar to the Capitol tomorrow?
CASCA: He doth; for he did bid Antonius
Send word to you he would be there tomorrow.
CICERO: Good night then, Casca; this disturbed sky   39
Is not to walk in.
CASCA: Farewell Cicero.   [*Exit Cicero*

Enter CASSIUS

CASSIUS: Who's there?
CASCA: A Roman.
CASSIUS: Casca, by your voice.
CASCA: Your ear is good. Cassius, what night is this!
CASSIUS: A very pleasing night to honest men.
CASCA: Who ever knew the heavens menace so?
CASSIUS: Those that have known the earth so full of faults.
For my part, I have walked about the streets,
Submitting me unto the perilous night;
And thus unbraced, Casca, as you see,
Have bared my bosom to the thunderstone;
And when the cross blue lightning seemed to open   50
The breast of heaven, I did present myself
Even in the aim and very flash of it.
CASCA: But wherefore did you so much tempt the heavens?
It is the part of men to fear and tremble,

56   *heralds*, forewarnings. *astonish*, dismay.

57   *dull*, stupid, dim-witted. Compare I. ii, 289–90. Cassius speaks scornfully to provoke Casca into joining the conspirators.

58   *want*, lack.

60   *cast . . . wonder*, throw yourself into a state of wonder.

61   *strange impatience*, unnatural restlessness.

62   *But . . . cause.* Cassius gives an interpretation of the portents to suit his own ends.

64   *from . . . kind*, change their character and nature (Arden).

65   *old . . . calculate.* Proverbial. *calculate*, prophesy.

66   *ordinance*, natural order.

67   *preformed*, inborn.

68   *monstrous*, unnatural, abnormal.

69   *infused . . . spirits*, filled them with such qualities.

71   *monstrous state*, unnatural state of things.

77   *personal action*, his deeds, or bodily powers. *prodigious*, ominous.

78   *fearful*, terrifying. *eruptions*, outbreaks in nature.

79   *'Tis . . . Cassius?* Is this question put furtively, for information, with surprise, or as confirming an opinion already formed?

82   *woe the while*, what a wretched age this is.

84   *yoke and sufferance*, our meek endurance of slavery.

When the most mighty gods by tokens send
Such dreadful heralds to astonish us.
CASSIUS: You are dull, Casca, and those sparks of life
  That should be in a Roman you do want,
  Or else you use not. You look pale, and gaze,
  And put on fear, and cast yourself in wonder,   60
  To see the strange impatience of the heavens.
  But if you would consider the true cause
  Why all these fires, why all these gliding ghosts,
  Why birds and beasts from quality and kind,
  Why old men, fools, and children calculate,
  Why all these things change from their ordinance,
  Their natures, and preformed faculties
  To monstrous quality,—why you shall find
  That heaven hath infused them with these spirits,
  To make them instruments of fear and warning   70
  Unto some monstrous state.
  Now could I, Casca, name to thee a man
  Most like this dreadful night,
  That thunders, lightens, opens graves, and roars
  As doth the lion in the Capitol;
  A man no mightier than thyself, or me,
  In personal action, yet prodigious grown,
  And fearful, as these strange eruptions are.
CASCA: 'Tis Cæsar that you mean, is it not, Cassius?
CASSIUS: Let it be who it is; for Romans now   80
  Have thews and limbs like to their ancestors;
  But, wóe the while, our fathers' minds are dead,
  And we are governed with our mothers' spirits:
  Our yoke and sufferance show us womanish.
CASCA: Indeed, they say the senators tomorrow
  Mean to establish Cæsar as a king;
  And he shall wear his crown by sea and land,
  In every place, save here in Italy.

89   *I . . . then*, i.e. he will sheathe it in his own body.

89–90 *I . . . Cassius.* What is Cassius' reaction to Casca's news? Is he—
      appalled, enraged, calm, passionate, thoughtful, boastful? Any
      gesture? Is his use of his name 'Cassius' arrogant?

95   *be . . . spirit*, imprison the resolute mind.

98   *know . . . world*, let all the world know.

102   *cancel*, (*a*) end (his life), (*b*) end an agreement or bond. The word is
      suggested by 'bondman'.

104   *Poor man.* Contemptuous.

106   *hinds*, (*a*) deer, (*b*) servants.

108   *trash*, twigs, kindling.

109   *offal*, wood chips, waste scraps.

110   *base*, (*a*) foundation, (*b*) vile.

111   *vile*, worthless.

111–5 *But . . . indifferent.* Spoken as if to himself for Casca to overhear.

113   *willing bondman*, i.e. Casca. A provocative piece of sarcasm.

114   *My . . . made*, I shall have to answer for what I have said. *armed*,
      prepared.

115   *indifferent*, of no concern.

116   *You . . . Casca.* Casca, proud of his integrity, is provoked into
      declaring his support for Cassius.

117   *fleering*, (*a*) fawning, (*b*) sneering. *Hold, my hand*, wait, here is my
      hand on it.

118   *Be factious*, be active, or, stir up others. *griefs*, grievances.

CASSIUS: I know where I will wear this dagger then;
　　　Cassius from bondage will deliver Cassius.　　　　90
　　　Therein, ye gods, you make the weak most strong;
　　　Therein, ye gods, you tyrants do defeat.
　　　Nor stony tower, nor walls of beaten brass,
　　　Nor airless dungeon, nor strong links of iron,
　　　Can be retentive to the strength of spirit;
　　　But life, being weary of these worldly bars,
　　　Never lacks power to dismiss itself.
　　　If I know this, know all the world besides,
　　　That part of tyranny that I do bear
　　　I can shake off at pleasure.　　　　　　　[*Thunder still*
CASCA:　　　　　　　　So can I.　　　　　　　100
　　　So every bondman in his own hand bears
　　　The power to cancel his captivity.
CASSIUS: And why should Cæsar be a tyrant then?
　　　Poor man, I know he would not be a wolf,
　　　But that he sees the Romans are but sheep;
　　　He were no lion, were not Romans hinds.
　　　Those that with haste will make a mighty fire
　　　Begin it with weak straws. What trash is Rome,
　　　What rubbish, and what offal, when it serves
　　　For the base matter to illuminate　　　　　　110
　　　So vile a thing as Cæsar! But, O grief,
　　　Where hast thou led me? I perhaps speak this
　　　Before a willing bondman; then I know
　　　My answer must be made. But I am armed,
　　　And dangers are to me indifferent.
CASCA: You speak to Casca, and to such a man
　　　That is no fleering tell-tale. Hold, my hand.
　　　Be factious for redress of all these griefs,
　　　And I will set this foot of mine as far
　　　As who goes farthest.
CASSIUS:　　　　　　There's a bargain made.　　　120

124   *honourable-dangerous.* See I. ii, 86.

      Cassius' tone changes swiftly from grief, l. 111, to rapid, confidential explanation. Is his vehemence and sorrow in ll. 103–15 genuine or hypocritical?

126   *Pompey's porch.* One of the porches adjoining the theatre built by Pompey in the Campus Martius outside the city.

128   *complexion . . . element,* state of the sky. *complexion,* physical make-up, temperament, depending on the four humours, 'hot, cold, moist, dry'. *element,* sky, atmosphere. The word was used for the four substances of which all things were believed to be made, earth, air, fire and water.

129   *In favour's like,* in appearance is like (Johnson) reading. Some editors prefer 'is favoured like' for the Folio reading 'is Favors, like'.

131   *Stand close,* step aside.

132   *his gait.* Should Cinna have a distinctive walk?

135   *incorporate,* one of our fellowship, joined.

137   *I . . . on't,* i.e. Casca's membership of the group.

142   *Be you content,* that is in hand, do not worry about that.

143   *prætor's chair.* Brutus, as prætor, dealt with complaints brought to him as he sat in an official chair.

144   *Where . . . it,* where only Brutus may find it.

145   *Set . . . wax,* i.e. fasten it with wax.

150   *hie,* hasten.

Now know you, Casca, I have moved already
Some certain of the noblest-minded Romans
To undergo with me an enterprise
Of honourable-dangerous consequence;
And I do know, by this, they stay for me
In Pompey's porch; for now, this fearful night,
There is no stir or walking in the streets;
And the complexion of the element
In favour's like the work we have in hand,
Most bloody, fiery, and most terrible.   130

Enter CINNA

CASCA: Stand close awhile, for here comes one in haste.
CASSIUS: 'Tis Cinna; I do know him by his gait;
   He is a friend. Cinna, where haste you so?
CINNA: To find out you. Who's that? Metellus Cimber?
CASSIUS: No, it is Casca, one incorporate
   To our attempts. Am I not stayed for, Cinna?
CINNA: I am glad on't. What a fearful night is this!
   There's two or three of us have seen strange sights.
CASSIUS: Am I not stayed for? Tell me.
CINNA: Yes, you are.
   O Cassius, if you could   140
   But win the noble Brutus to our party—
CASSIUS: Be you content. Good Cinna, take this paper,
   And look you lay it in the prætor's chair,
   Where Brutus may but find it. And throw this
   In at his window. Set this up with wax
   Upon old Brutus' statue. All this done,
   Repair to Pompey's porch, where you shall find us.
   Is Decius Brutus and Trebonius there?
CINNA: All but Metellus Cimber, and he's gone
   To seek you at your house. Well, I will hie,   150
   And so bestow these papers as you bade me.

65

154–   *Three . . . him.* Is Brutus being used as a catspaw, a friend, a man of
64   honour, an equal, a figurehead, a dupe?

156   *encounter,* meeting.

159   *countenance,* (*a*) face, (*b*) support, approval. *richest alchemy.* Alche-
mists sought vainly to change base metals into gold. An ironic
forecast of their lack of success.

162   *right well conceited,* (*a*) aptly expressed, (*b*) exactly judged.

CASSIUS: That done, repair to Pompey's theatre.   [*Exit Cinna*
　　　Come Casca, you and I will yet ere day
　　　See Brutus at his house. Three parts of him
　　　Is ours already, and the man entire
　　　Upon the next encounter yields him ours.
CASCA: O he sits high in all the people's hearts;
　　　And that which would appear offence in us,
　　　His countenance, like richest alchemy,
　　　Will change to virtue and to worthiness.   160
CASSIUS: Him and his worth, and our great need of him
　　　You have right well conceited. Let us go,
　　　For it is after midnight; and ere day
　　　We will awake him, and be sure of him.   [*Exeunt*

The disorder in the heavens corresponds with the disorder in Brutus' mind. The part of Lucius and the references to light have a symbolic value.

> *Orchard*, garden.

2-3　*I . . . day.* The storm has obscured the stars. Brutus in darkness in his orchard represents also the obscurity and loss of direction in his mind.

4　*I . . . soundly.* The innocent sleep of the boy Lucius contrasts with the wakeful inner conflict of his master. Some have seen in the aptly named Lucius, Brutus' good angel, the bringer of light.

5　*When,* quickly.

7　*Get . . . study.* Brutus seeks for light and contemplation within the security of his study, but he never reaches it. In this scene his reflections are constantly interrupted. *taper,* candle.

10-34　*It . . . shell.* Brutus' speech falls into three parts: three proverb-like statements on which he bases his thought, and three acknowledgements of Cæsar's good character hitherto. The three parts may be brought out by movement, gesture, and variation in speed and tone of speaking.

10　*It . . . death.* Is this short, terrible sentence spoken as a decisive conclusion, a proposition to be debated, an end to be explained away?

11　*spurn,* strike, kick.

12　*the general,* the public good. *would be,* wishes to be.

14-15　*It . . . walking,* the bright power of the sun hatches the poisonous snake that threatens passers-by, i.e. a good thing may produce evil.

15　*Crown him that,* i.e. crown him king (Sisson). Some editors alter to 'Crown him?—that;—'. To Brutus the word 'king' is distasteful. (See l. 54.)

15-21　*Crown . . . reason,* i.e. if we crown him he will have absolute power, which, corrupted, may become tyrannical and pitiless; although it is true that Cæsar has not allowed his feelings to have more control over his actions than his reason has.

16　*sting,* fang, weapon.

17　*danger,* harm, injury.

18-19　*The . . . power,* the wrongful use of authority is when in the exercise of its power it shuts out pity.

ACT TWO

SCENE ONE

Enter BRUTUS

BRUTUS: What Lucius, ho!
  I cannot, by the progress of the stars,
  Give guess how near to day. Lucius I say!
  I would it were my fault to sleep so soundly.
  When Lucius, when? Awake, I say! What Lucius!

Enter LUCIUS

LUCIUS: Called you my lord?
BRUTUS: Get me a taper in my study, Lucius:
  When it is lighted, come and call me here.
LUCIUS: I will my lord.   [*Exit*
BRUTUS: It must be by his death; and for my part,   10
  I know no personal cause to spurn at him,
  But for the general. He would be crowned.
  How that might change his nature, there's the question.
  It is the bright day that brings forth the adder,
  And that craves wary walking. Crown him that,
  And then I grant we put a sting in him,
  That at his will he may do danger with.
  Th' abuse of greatness is, when it disjoins
  Remorse from power; and to speak truth of Cæsar,

20   *affections*, feelings, passions. *swayed*, ruled.

21   *common proof*, (*a*) a rhetorical device for augmenting a speech, (*b*) common experience.

22   *lowliness*, pretended humbleness. *young ambition's*, ambitious young man's.

24   *round*, rung.

26   *base*, (*a*) low, (*b*) servile. *degrees*, (*a*) steps, (*b*) offices, ranks.

28   *prevent*, forestall. *quarrel*, cause for complaint.

29   *colour*, excuse.

30   *Fashion it thus*, put it in the way I have just shown. *augmented*, i.e. increased by the addition of the 'common proof'. A rhetorical term.

32–3 *And . . . mischievous*. See ll. 14–15.

33   *kind*, nature. *mischievous*, dangerous.

36–8 See I. ii, 309–14.

40   *ides of March*. The Folio has 'first of March'. This is possibly a slip by the compositor who read '1st' for ides, or a slip by Shakespeare who put down the date of the Senate's meeting in Plutarch, forgetting that he was concentrating these events into 14 and 15 March. The reminder of the date serves an obvious dramatic purpose; it again links Brutus and Cæsar. See I. ii, 19, and IV. iii, 18.

44   *exhalations*, meteors. It was believed that meteors were drawn up as vapours from the earth by the sun. A baleful light by which to read!

46   *Brutus . . . awake*. i.e. Brutus is inactive.

I have not known when his affections swayed   20
More than his reason. But 'tis a common proof,
That lowliness is young ambition's ladder,
Whereto the climber-upward turns his face;
But when he once attains the upmost round,
He then unto the ladder turns his back,
Looks in the clouds, scorning the base degrees
By which he did ascend. So Cæsar may;
Then lest he may, prevent. And, since the quarrel
Will bear no colour for the thing he is,
Fashion it thus: that what he is, augmented,   30
Would run to these and these extremities.
And therefore think him as a serpent's egg,
Which hatched, would as his kind, grow mischievous,
And kill him in the shell.

Re-enter LUCIUS

LUCIUS: The taper burneth in your closet sir.
　　Searching the window for a flint, I found
　　This paper, thus sealed up; and I am sure
　　It did not lie there when I went to bed.　　*[Gives him the letter*
BRUTUS: Get you to bed again, it is not day.
　　Is not tomorrow, boy, the ides of March?   40
LUCIUS: I know not sir.
BRUTUS: Look in the calendar, and bring me word.
LUCIUS: I will sir.　　　　　　　　　　　　　　　　*[Exit*
BRUTUS: The exhalations whizzing in the air
　　Gives so much light that I may read by them.
　　　　　　　　　　　　[Opens the letter and reads
　　'Brutus, thou sleep'st; awake, and see thyself.
　　Shall Rome, &c. Speak, strike, redress.'
　　'Brutus, thou sleep'st: awake!'
　　Such instigations have been often dropped
　　Where I have took them up.   50

71

54   *Tarquin.* See note I. ii, 159.

56–8   *O . . . Brutus.* Brutus makes his decision. Any change in his voice, any gesture?

57   *If . . . follow,* if it is certain that matters will be put right by this means.

57–8   *thou . . . petition,* you will obtain your desire in full.

61   *whet,* (*a*) urge, (*b*) sharpen—as a knife.

64   *motion,* prompting, proposal, impulse.

65   *phantasma,* nightmare.

66–9   *The . . . insurrection.* Several explanations have been offered. 'Genius' may mean the soul. The general meaning then would be that the senses ('mortal instruments') are exerting a corrupt influence on the soul which struggles to resist. Alternatively 'genius' may mean evil spirit or bad angel, which, having driven away the good angel is directing the reluctant bodily organs to commit murder. Finally 'genius' may mean Brutus' guardian spirit which is under the evil influence of Cassius' stronger genius, and this too gives rise to strife between spirit and body.

69   *insurrection.* See I. ii, 46.

70   *brother.* Cassius had married Brutus' sister, Junia.

72   *moe,* more.

75   *discover them,* find out who they are.

76   *favour,* appearance, features.

'Shall Rome &c.' Thus must I piece it out:
Shall Rome stand under one man's awe? What, Rome?
My ancestors did from the streets of Rome
The Tarquin drive, when he was called a king.
'Speak, strike, redress.' Am I entreated
To speak and strike? O Rome, I make thee promise,
If the redress will follow, thou receivest
Thy full petition at the hand of Brutus.

Re-enter LUCIUS

LUCIUS: Sir, March is wasted fifteen days.   [*Knocking within*
BRUTUS: 'Tis good. Go to the gate; somebody knocks.

[*Exit Lucius*

Since Cassius first did whet me against Cæsar,   61
I have not slept.
Between the acting of a dreadful thing
And the first motion, all the interim is
Like a phantasma, or a hideous dream.
The genius and the mortal instruments
Are then in council; and the state of man,
Like to a little kingdom, suffers then
The nature of an insurrection.

Re-enter LUCIUS

LUCIUS: Sir, 'tis your brother Cassius at the door,   70
Who doth desire to see you.
BRUTUS: Is he alone?
LUCIUS: No sir, there are moe with him.
BRUTUS: Do you know them?
LUCIUS: No sir, their hats are plucked about their ears,
And half their faces buried in their cloaks,
That by no means I may discover them
By any mark of favour.
BRUTUS: Let 'em enter.   [*Exit Lucius*

83   *put thy.* See l. 225. Some editors prefer the reading of the Second Folio 'path, thy' (path = walk, journey), but the use of 'path' in this way is extremely rare. *native semblance*, natural appearance.

84   *Erebus.* In classical myth a place of darkness between Earth and Hades.

85   *prevention*, discovery and forestalling.

86   *I . . . rest.* Brutus has uttered his soliloquy from the front of the stage. Is he surprised at their entry, annoyed at the intrusion, discourteous in his lack of greeting? *too bold*, intruding.

94–7   *He is welcome.* How does Brutus greet each man? (See l. 112.)

98   *watchful cares*, cares that keep one awake.

100   *Shall . . . word?* What does Cassius say to Brutus—does he vouch for the reliability of the other conspirators, or inquire whether Brutus has decided to join them?

101–   *Here . . . here.* What is the dramatic value of this conversation—to
11   dissipate their nervous tension by talking about something trivial, to avoid talking about serious matters in the absence of Brutus and Cassius and to fill in time, to symbolize the inability of the conspirators to see the right way, to give Shakespeare an opportunity of scene painting?

104   *fret*, adorn, interlace.

They are the faction. O conspiracy,
Sham'st thou to show thy dangerous brow by night,
When evils are most free? O then, by day
Where wilt thou find a cavern dark enough   80
To mask thy monstrous visage? Seek none, conspiracy;
Hide it in smiles and affability.
For if thou put thy native semblance on,
Not Erebus itself were dim enough
To hide thee from prevention.

Enter the conspirators, CASSIUS, CASCA, DECIUS, CINNA,
        METELLUS CIMBER, *and* TREBONIUS

CASSIUS: I think we are too bold upon your rest.
  Good morrow Brutus; do we trouble you?
BRUTUS: I have been up this hour, awake all night.
  Know I these men that come along with you?
CASSIUS: Yes, every man of them; and no man here   90
  But honours you; and every one doth wish
  You had but that opinion of yourself
  Which every noble Roman bears of you.
  This is Trebonius.
BRUTUS: He is welcome hither.
CASSIUS: This, Decius Brutus.
BRUTUS: He is welcome too.
CASSIUS: This, Casca; this, Cinna; and this, Metellus Cimber.
BRUTUS: They are all welcome.
  What watchful cares do interpose themselves
  Betwixt your eyes and night?
CASSIUS: Shall I entreat a word?   [*Brutus and Cassius whisper*
DECIUS: Here lies the east. Doth not the day break here?   101
CASCA: No.
CINNA: O pardon sir, it doth; and yon grey lines
  That fret the clouds are messengers of day.
CASCA: You shall confess that you are both deceived.

107   *a . . . south*, some distance towards the south.

108   *Weighing*, considering.

112   *all over*, all of you again, or, all in turn.

114–   Brutus over-rules Cassius and the others on three occasions during
   40 this scene (see ll. 150, 162). Is Brutus—awkward, opinionated,
       idealistic, uncompromising, honourable, unpractical, incon-
       siderate?

114–   *If . . . weak*, if the anxiety and misery in men's faces, the suffering
   16 of their souls, the evils of the time are not strong enough motives.
       Sisson refers the passage to ll. 74, 78 and interprets: 'Are not these
       motives enough, that our souls suffer, that we live in corrupt and
       evil days, that even men's faces dare not appear openly, and men
       dare not be themselves.' Other editors suggest 'faith' or 'fate' for
       'face'.

117   *idle bed*, (*a*) empty bed, (*b*) idly to bed. Contemptuous phrase.

118   *high-sighted*, ambitious, or perhaps a metaphor from falconry
       (see I. i, 74–5) and hence, 'soaring almost above the view of men
       select its prey and swoop on it' (Arden). Tyranny in Ripa's
       emblems is represented as a woman standing in order by her
       watchfulness to crush her enemies. Hence 'high-sighted' might
       mean overseeing, vigilant.

119   *by lottery*, by chance, i.e. as the tyrant's gaze chances to light on
       him (Arden). *these*, i.e. motives.

120–1 *bear . . . valour*. For the fire-kindle-steel image see I. ii, 176–7.

124   *prick*, urge.

125   *secret Romans*, discreet Romans or deep in our hearts we are true
       Romans.

126   *palter*, quibble, deceive.

127–8 *honesty . . . it*, honourable men giving their word to each other to
       undertake this enterprise or die in the attempt.

129   *Swear*, let . . . swear oaths. *cautelous*, cunning, deceitful.

130   *carrions*, living carcasses, skeletons. *suffering*, cringing, submissive.

133   *even*, untroubled.

134   *insuppressive*, indomitable, undaunted.

135   *To think*, by thinking.

138   *a several bastardy*, a separate, individual act showing it to be not
       true Roman blood.

Here, as I point my sword, the sun arises,
Which is a great way growing on the south,
Weighing the youthful season of the year.
Some two months hence, up higher toward the north
He first presents his fire; and the high east   110
Stands, as the Capitol, directly here.
BRUTUS: Give me your hands all over, one by one.
CASSIUS: And let us swear our resolution.
BRUTUS: No, not an oath. If not the face of men,
The sufferance of our souls, the time's abuse—
If these be motives weak, break off betimes,
And every man hence to his idle bed.
So let high-sighted tyranny range on,
Till each man drop by lottery. But if these,
As I am sure they do, bear fire enough   120
To kindle cowards, and to steel with valour
The melting spirits of women, then, countrymen,
What need we any spur but our own cause,
To prick us to redress? What other bond
Than secret Romans, that have spoke the word,
And will not palter? And what other oath
Than honesty to honesty engaged,
That this shall be, or we will fall for it?
Swear priests and cowards, and men cautelous,
Old feeble carrions, and such suffering souls   130
That welcome wrongs; unto bad causes swear
Such creatures as men doubt; but do not stain
The even virtue of our enterprise,
Nor th' insuppressive mettle of our spirits,
To think that or our cause or our performance
Did need an oath; when every drop of blood
That every Roman bears, and nobly bears,
Is guilty of a several bastardy,
If he do break the smallest particle

144-6   *for . . . deeds.* Note the extension and shifting of an image: silver—
          purchase—good opinions—buy voices—commend.

145   *opinion*, reputation.

146   *voices*, support, approval.

147   *judgement . . . hands.* Parallels 'his silver hairs' and 'our deeds'.

148-9   *wildness . . . gravity.* Perhaps a Christian thought. See *Romans*, vi.
         4-7.

149   *gravity*, A quibble on 'grave'. Compare *2 Henry IV*, V. ii, 123-4.
         Is Metellus serious, mocking, cynical?

150-2   *O . . . begin.* This is the second of three occasions in this scene
         when Brutus over-rules the opinion of Cassius and the others.

150   *break with him*, break our news to him, let him into our affairs.

151-2   *For . . . begin.* Does this imply that Cicero is—obstinate, ambi-
         tious, distrustful, egoistic, intellectually snobbish, wayward?

153   *Indeed . . . fit.* Casca in l. 142 had another opinion of him. Is he one
         who cannot bear argument, does not know his own mind,
         petulant, impatient, inconsistent, anxious to agree?

156-7   *so . . . Cæsar.* Grimly ironic, i.e. their love is so great that it would
         be natural for them to die together.

158   *shrewd*, dangerous, cunning. *contriver*, plotter, conspirator. *means*,
         powers.

160   *annoy*, injure, harm. *prevent*, forestall.

162   *Our . . . bloody.* The third over-ruling of others' suggestions.

164   *wrath in death*, killing with savagery. *envy*, spite, hatred.

165   *limb*, hanger-on.

166   *sacrificers.* Brutus seeks to dignify the murder as an offering to the
         gods (see l. 173).

167   *spirit of Cæsar*, i.e. what Cæsar stands for. See IV. iii, 275-87;
         V. iii, 94-6 for a change in Cæsar's 'spirit'.

168   *And . . . blood.* In Elizabethan belief the blood contained the spirits.
         Here there is an echo of that belief attached to another meaning of
         'spirit', soul.

Of any promise that hath passed from him. 140

CASSIUS: But what of Cicero? Shall we sound him?
　　I think he will stand very strong with us.

CASCA: Let us not leave him out.

CINNA: 　　　　　　　　　No, by no means.

METELLUS: O let us have him, for his silver hairs
　　Will purchase us a good opinion
　　And buy men's voices to commend our deeds.
　　It shall be said his judgement ruled our hands;
　　Our youths and wildness shall no whit appear,
　　But all be buried in his gravity.

BRUTUS: O name him not; let us not break with him; 150
　　For he will never follow any thing
　　That other men begin.

CASSIUS: 　　　　　　　Then leave him out.

CASCA: Indeed he is not fit.

DECIUS: Shall no man else be touched but only Cæsar?

CASSIUS: Decius, well urged. I think it is not meet,
　　Mark Antony, so well beloved of Cæsar,
　　Should outlive Cæsar. We shall find of him
　　A shrewd contriver; and you know, his means,
　　If he improve them, may well stretch so far
　　As to annoy us all; which to prevent, 160
　　Let Antony and Cæsar fall together.

BRUTUS: Our course will seem too bloody, Caius Cassius,
　　To cut the head off, and then hack the limbs,
　　Like wrath in death, and envy afterwards;
　　For Antony is but a limb of Cæsar.
　　Let us be sacrificers, but not butchers, Caius.
　　We all stand up against the spirit of Cæsar,
　　And in the spirit of men there is no blood:
　　O that we then could come by Cæsar's spirit,
　　And not dismember Cæsar! But alas, 170
　　Cæsar must bleed for it. And gentle friends,

173   *carve . . . gods*, kill him with ceremony as an offering to the gods, i.e. as a deer was cut up.

174   *Not . . . hounds*, i.e. not as a fox whose carcass was thrown to the hounds

175-7   *And . . . 'em*, let our mind excite our feelings and limbs to a deed of murder and afterwards rebuke them. Compare the comments of Henry IV on the murder of Richard II, *Richard II*, V. vi, 34–44.

177-8   *This . . . envious*, this will make it clear that our motives arose from necessity not from hatred.

180   *purgers*, healers, i.e. by bleeding—a common medical practice.

183   *Yet*. What does Cassius imply?

184   *ingrafted*, deep-rooted. Cassius extends the limb (branch) image.

185   *Alas . . . him*. A kindly meant, irritatingly patronizing sweeping aside of Cassius' views. What actions are appropriate during the course of the speech?

186-7   *If . . . Cæsar*. Brutus adapts Cassius' grim suggestion ll. 155–7.

187   *take thought*, give way to sorrow.

188   *that . . . should*, that is too much to expect of him.

190   *no fear in*, nothing to fear from.

     How do the conspirators respond to Brutus' speech? Are they convinced by it or not?

191   *For . . . hereafter*. Does this suggest that Antony is—shallow, time-serving, immature, trivial, contemptible, sensible?

     Is Trebonius—a jovial blusterer, an optimist, a wishful thinker; superficial, over confident?

     Are the conspirators disputing or applauding Trebonius' remarks so that Brutus has to call for silence? Is it important that the audience should know the time? It leads naturally to a change of subject.

195-7   *For . . . ceremonies*. Is this a sign of Cæsar's declining faculties, or a device to increase suspense in II. ii, 55–6?

196   *main*, strong, convinced.

197   *fantasy*, imaginings. *ceremonies*, portents, omens.

198   *apparent prodigies*, wonders that have appeared.

200   *augurers*, augurs. Priests who interpreted omens.

Let's kill him boldly, but not wrathfully;
Let's carve him as a dish fit for the gods,
Not hew him as a carcass fit for hounds.
And let our hearts, as subtle masters do,
Stir up their servants to an act of rage,
And after seem to chide 'em. This shall make
Our purpose necessary, and not envious;
Which so appearing to the common eyes,
We shall be called purgers, not murderers.   180
And for Mark Antony, think not of him;
For he can do no more than Cæsar's arm
When Cæsar's head is off.

CASSIUS: Yet I fear him;
    For in the ingrafted love he bears to Cæsar—
BRUTUS: Alas good Cassius, do not think of him.
    If he love Cæsar, all that he can do
    Is to himself, take thought, and die for Cæsar.
    And that were much he should; for he is given
    To sports, to wildness, and much company.
TREBONIUS: There is no fear in him; let him not die,   190
    For he will live, and laugh at this hereafter.   [*Clock strikes*
BRUTUS: Peace, count the clock.
CASSIUS: The clock hath stricken three.
TREBONIUS: 'Tis time to part.
CASSIUS: But it is doubtful yet,
    Whether Cæsar will come forth today or no;
    For he is superstitious grown of late,
    Quite from the main opinion he held once
    Of fantasy, of dreams, and ceremonies.
    It may be, these apparent prodigies,
    The unaccustomed terror of this night,
    And the persuasion of his augurers,   200
    May hold him from the Capitol today.
DECIUS: Never fear that. If he be so resolved,

81

204   *unicorns . . . trees.* In medieval story the hunter stood in front of a tree, and when charged by a unicorn stepped aside at the last moment, whereupon the unicorn's horn was driven immovably into the tree, and the animal was then captured.

205   *bears with glasses,* i.e. by means of mirrors. Another belief similar to the last was that the bear seeing its reflection in pieces of broken mirror imagined that it saw a cub and paused long enough to be caught. *elephants with holes,* by means of pits lightly covered over so that the elephant falls in.

206   *toils,* snares or nets. *men with flatterers.* Emphatic.

    Decius' point is that as these mighty animals are betrayed by their own incaution, so a man is deceived by flatterers.

    Is Decius' description received by the others in silence, with laughter, or with approval?

210   *give . . . bent,* guide his mood into the right channel.

213   *uttermost,* latest.

215–   *Caius . . . him.* Does this suggest amateurish plotting rather than a
17   carefully thought out conspiracy?

215   *bear Cæsar hard,* bears a grudge against Cæsar.

216   *rated,* denounced, angrily reproached.

218   *by him,* by his house.

225   *Let . . . purposes,* do not let our faces reveal our intentions.

227   *untired spirits,* unwearying zest. *formal constancy,* steadfast bearing.

229   *Boy . . . asleep?* Where is Lucius?

230–3   *Enjoy . . . sound.* Again Brutus draws the contrast of his own state of mind with Lucius' innocence.

230   *honey-heavy . . . slumber,* sweet refreshment of deep sleep.

231   *figures,* shapes, pictures. *fantasies,* illusions.

233   *Brutus my lord.* Are Portia's tones casual, despairing, alarmed, frantic, tearful, anxious? Accordingly how should she enter?

I can o'ersway him; for he loves to hear
That unicorns may be betrayed with trees,
And bears with glasses, elephants with holes,
Lions with toils, and men with flatterers;
But when I tell him he hates flatterers,
He says he does, being then most flattered.
Let me work;
For I can give his humour the true bent,   210
And I will bring him to the Capitol.

CASSIUS: Nay, we will all of us be there to fetch him.

BRUTUS: By the eighth hour; is that the uttermost?

CINNA: Be that the uttermost, and fail not then.

METELLUS: Caius Ligarius doth bear Cæsar hard,
  Who rated him for speaking well of Pompey;
  I wonder none of you have thought of him.

BRUTUS: Now good Metellus, go along by him.
  He loves me well, and I have given him reasons.
  Send him but hither, and I'll fashion him.   220

CASSIUS: The morning comes upon's. We'll leave you, Brutus.
  And friends disperse yourselves; but all remember
  What you have said, and show yourselves true Romans.

BRUTUS: Good gentlemen, look fresh and merrily.
  Let not our looks put on our purposes,
  But bear it as our Roman actors do,
  With untired spirits and formal constancy;
  And so good morrow to you everyone.   [*Exeunt all but Brutus*
Boy! Lucius! Fast asleep? It is no matter;
Enjoy the honey-heavy dew of slumber.   230
Thou hast no figures nor no fantasies,
Which busy care draws in the brains of men;
Therefore thou sleep'st so sound.

Enter PORTIA

PORTIA: Brutus my lord.

234-6 *Portia . . . morning.* Is Brutus surprised, alarmed, indignant, angry, tender, solicitous?

236 *weak condition*, delicate constitution.

237 *ungently*, discourteously.

240 *with . . . across.* A sign of melancholy.

250 *effect of humour*, result of ill-humour (i.e. unbalanced proportions of the four humours that were thought to determine a man's temperament: blood, phlegm, choler, melancholy).

253 *shape*, appearance.

254 *condition*, state of mind.

255 *Brutus*, to be Brutus.

257 *I . . . all.* Is Brutus—impatient, abrupt, tense, a poor liar?

258-9 *Brutus . . . it.* A tactful way of exposing a lie.

260 *Why . . . bed.* Is Brutus—irritable, coaxing, petulant, restive, pleading?

261 *physical*, healthy.

262 *unbraced*, with doublet unfastened and open. A sign of melancholy and a disturbed mind. *suck . . . humours*, breathe in the moist air.

263 *What . . . sick?* Gently ironic.

265 *vile contagion*, filthy diseases.

266 *tempt*, risk. *rheumy*, causing colds. *unpurged*, i.e. by the sun that drove away mists.

BRUTUS: Portia! What mean you? Wherefore rise you now?
　　It is not for your health thus to commit
　　Your weak condition to the raw cold morning.
PORTIA: Nor for yours neither. Y'have ungently, Brutus,
　　Stole from my bed: and yesternight at supper
　　You suddenly arose, and walked about,
　　Musing and sighing, with your arms across;　　　　　　240
　　And when I asked you what the matter was,
　　You stared upon me with ungentle looks.
　　I urged you further; then you scratched your head,
　　And too impatiently stamped with your foot.
　　Yet I insisted, yet you answered not,
　　But with an angry wafture of your hand
　　Gave sign for me to leave you. So I did,
　　Fearing to strengthen that impatience
　　Which seemed too much enkindled, and withal
　　Hoping it was but an effect of humour,　　　　　　　250
　　Which sometime hath his hour with every man.
　　It will not let you eat, nor talk, nor sleep;
　　And could it work so much upon your shape,
　　As it hath much prevailed on your condition,
　　I should not know you Brutus. Dear my lord,
　　Make me acquainted with your cause of grief.
BRUTUS: I am not well in health, and that is all.
PORTIA: Brutus is wise, and were he not in health,
　　He would embrace the means to come by it.
BRUTUS: Why so I do. Good Portia go to bed.　　　　　260
PORTIA: Is Brutus sick, and is it physical
　　To walk unbraced and suck up the humours
　　Of the dank morning? What, is Brutus sick?
　　And will he steal out of his wholesome bed,
　　To dare the vile contagion of the night,
　　And tempt the rheumy and unpurged air,
　　To add unto his sickness? No my Brutus,

268   *sick offence,* hurtful illness.

271   *charm,* (*a*) beg, (*b*) put a charm upon, i.e. with her beauty.

274   *half,* wife.

275   *heavy,* sad, dejected.

277–8 *who . . . darkness.* An echo of Brutus' words, ll. 77–81, and what they imply.

280,   *bond, excepted, limitation,* a common thought unites these words,
1, 3   they are 'legal terms of land-tenure' (Wilson). The thought perhaps continues in 'Dwell . . . suburbs'.

281   *excepted,* i.e. excluded by a clause in a contract.

283   *in sort,* in part. *limitation.* Period stated for the continuance of an estate, fixed period.

285   *suburbs.* London suburbs were notoriously the haunt of harlots or loose women.

       How does Brutus receive Portia's conclusion? Is he shocked, amused, deeply moved, playful, patronizing, sincere? Any movement or gesture?

295   *Cato's daughter.* Cato, the elder, was famous for the stern uprightness of his life. Defeated by Cæsar in Africa, he committed suicide rather than be taken prisoner.

299   *strong proof,* severe test.

You have some sick offence within your mind,
Which, by the right and virtue of my place,
I ought to know of: and upon my knees,   270
I charm you, by my once commended beauty,
By all your vows of love, and that great vow
Which did incorporate and make us one,
That you unfold to me, your self, your half,
Why you are heavy, and what men tonight
Have had resort to you; for here have been
Some six or seven, who did hide their faces
Even from darkness.
BRUTUS: Kneel not, gentle Portia.
PORTIA: I should not need, if you were gentle Brutus.
    Within the bond of marriage, tell me Brutus,   280
    Is it excepted I should know no secrets
    That appertain to you? Am I your self
    But as it were in sort or limitation,
    To keep with you at meals, comfort your bed,
    And talk to you sometimes? Dwell I but in the suburbs
    Of your good pleasure? If it be no more,
    Portia is Brutus' harlot, not his wife.
BRUTUS: You are my true and honourable wife,
    As dear to me as are the ruddy drops
    That visit my sad heart.   290
PORTIA: If this were true, then should I know this secret.
    I grant I am a woman; but withal
    A woman that Lord Brutus took to wife.
    I grant I am a woman; but withal
    A woman well-reputed, Cato's daughter.
    Think you I am no stronger than my sex,
    Being so fathered, and so husbanded?
    Tell me your counsels, I will not disclose 'em.
    I have made strong proof of my constancy,
    Giving myself a voluntary wound   300

302–3   *O . . . wife.* A cry from the heart. Brutus at a moment of greatest emotion is interrupted by startling knocking.

307   *construe*, explain, translate.

308   *charactery . . . brows*, what is written on my sad brows; i.e. what causes the lines of worry on my forehead.

      What words apply to Portia—intelligent, courageous, masterful, frank, direct, proud, loving, resolute, domineering, tender, fanatic, manly?

      Is Caius Ligarius' entry an anti-climax, a collapse of tension, or sinister?

312   *how?* i.e. this is a surprise.

313   *Vouchsafe*, please accept. *feeble tongue*. How does Ligarius speak?

315   *wear a kerchief*, be ill.

322   *derived . . . loins*, descended from honourable ancestors.

323   *exorcist*, one who calls up spirits by magical rites.

324   *mortified*, dead.

327   *make . . . whole*, Brutus plays on Ligarius' thought, i.e. relieve the sufferers under Cæsar's rule. What is the dramatic value of this Ligarius episode: to enhance Brutus' powers of inspiring devotion with a faint echo of a New Testament miracle, to balance by contrast the scene with Portia, by symbolism to make an ironic comment on the sickness of the conspiracy, to sweep Brutus deeper into the conspiracy?

Here in the thigh. Can I bear that with patience,
And not my husband's secrets?

BRUTUS: O ye gods,
  Render me worthy of this noble wife!   [*Knocking within*
  Hark, hark, one knocks. Portia go in awhile,
  And by and by thy bosom shall partake
  The secrets of my heart.
  All my engagements I will construe to thee,
  All the charactery of my sad brows.
  Leave me with haste. [*Exit Portia*] Lucius, who's that knocks?

Re-enter LUCIUS *with* LIGARIUS

LUCIUS: Here is a sick man that would speak with you.   310
BRUTUS: Caius Ligarius, that Metellus spake of.
  Boy, stand aside. Caius Ligarius, how?
LIGARIUS: Vouchsafe good morrow from a feeble tongue.
BRUTUS: O what a time have you chose out brave Caius,
  To wear a kerchief! Would you were not sick!
LIGARIUS: I am not sick, if Brutus have in hand
  Any exploit worthy the name of honour.
BRUTUS: Such an exploit have I in hand Ligarius,
  Had you a healthful ear to hear of it.
LIGARIUS: By all the gods that Romans bow before,   320
  I here discard my sickness. Soul of Rome,
  Brave son, derived from honourable loins,
  Thou like an exorcist hast conjured up
  My mortified spirit. Now bid me run,
  And I will strive with things impossible,
  Yea get the better of them. What's to do?
BRUTUS: A piece of work that will make sick men whole.
LIGARIUS: But are not some whole that we must make sick?
BRUTUS: That must we also. What it is, my Caius,
  I shall unfold to thee, as we are going   330
  To whom it must be done.

Cæsar's House

The sudden renewal of the storm over Cæsar's home is an effective reminder of its omens and symbolism.

S.D.   *nightgown*, dressing gown.

1   *Nor . . . tonight.* Heavily ironic.

5   *present*, immediate.

6   *success*, result.
         Is Calphurnia's entrance agitated, calm, dignified, frenzied, anxious? Does she plead, give orders, or express fear?

10-12   *Cæsar . . . Cæsar.* It has been suggested that when Cæsar refers to himself by the name Cæsar he means the public figure as distinct from the private individual. Is he pompous, frightened, dignified, factual, boasting?

11   *Ne'er . . . back*, only showed themselves behind my back.

13   *stood on ceremonies*, considered omens and portents of any significance.

16   *horrid*, fearful, terrifying. *watch*, watchmen.

LIGARIUS: Set on your foot,
  And with a heart new-fired I follow you,
  To do I know not what; but it sufficeth
  That Brutus leads me on.
BRUTUS: Follow me then.   [*Exeunt*

SCENE TWO

Thunder and lightning. Enter CÆSAR *in his nightgown*

CÆSAR: Nor heaven nor earth have been at peace tonight.
  Thrice hath Calphurnia in her sleep cried out,
  'Help ho, they murder Cæsar!' Who's within?

Enter a SERVANT

SERVANT: My lord.
CÆSAR: Go bid the priests do present sacrifice,
  And bring me their opinions of success.
SERVANT: I will my lord.   [*Exit*

Enter CALPHURNIA

CALPHURNIA: What mean you Cæsar? Think you to walk forth?
  You shall not stir out of your house today.
CÆSAR: Cæsar shall forth. The things that threatened me   10
  Ne'er looked but on my back; when they shall see
  The face of Cæsar, they are vanished.
CALPHURNIA: Cæsar, I never stood on ceremonies,
  Yet now they fright me. There is one within,
  Besides the things that we have heard and seen,
  Recounts most horrid sights seen by the watch.
  A lioness hath whelped in the streets,
  And graves have yawned, and yielded up their dead;

19–22 *Fierce . . . air.* This description may have been inspired by a similar account in Ovid's *Metamorphoses, Bk. XV.* Its dramatic value is to intensify the awe and grandeur of Cæsar's overthrow.

19 *fought.* Some editors retain the Folio reading 'fight'.

20 *right . . . war,* correct battle order.

22 *hurtled,* clashed, crashed.

25 *beyond all use,* outside all experience, completely unnatural. Does Calphurnia stand still, cling to Cæsar, sob, make any other movement or gesture?

28 *Yet,* still.

29 *Are . . . general,* apply as much to other men.

31 *blaze forth,* (*a*) flame (a comet was normally called a 'blazing star'), (*b*) declare (as by a trumpet).

32–7 *Cowards . . . come.* Is this boastful, courageous, serene, resolute, pompous, arrogant, reflective?

36 *necessary,* inevitable.

39 *Plucking.* The technical word for drawing out the heart, liver, etc., of an animal.

42 *without a heart,* i.e. without courage.

46 *are.* The Folio has 'heare'. Some editors read 'were'. *littered,* born. Is Cæsar boastful, bragging, pompous, keeping up his courage, angry?

Fierce fiery warriors fought upon the clouds
In ranks and squadrons and right form of war,   20
Which drizzled blood upon the Capitol.
The noise of battle hurtled in the air;
Horses did neigh, and dying men did groan,
And ghosts did shriek and squeal about the streets.
O Cæsar, these things are beyond all use,
And I do fear them.

CÆSAR: What can be avoided
  Whose end is purposed by the mighty gods?
  Yet Cæsar shall go forth; for these predictions
  Are to the world in general as to Cæsar.

CALPHURNIA: When beggars die, there are no comets seen;   30
  The heavens themselves blaze forth the death of princes.

CÆSAR: Cowards die many times before their deaths,
  The valiant never taste of death but once.
  Of all the wonders that I yet have heard,
  It seems to me most strange that men should fear,
  Seeing that death, a necessary end,
  Will come when it will come.

Enter SERVANT

                        What say the augurers?
SERVANT: They would not have you to stir forth today.
  Plucking the entrails of an offering forth,
  They could not find a heart within the beast.   40

CÆSAR: The gods do this in shame of cowardice.
  Cæsar should be a beast without a heart
  If he should stay at home today for fear.
  No, Cæsar shall not. Danger knows full well
  That Cæsar is more dangerous than he.
  We are two lions littered in one day,
  And I the elder and more terrible.
  And Cæsar shall go forth.

49 *consumed in confidence*, swallowed up by your self-confidence.

50-3 *Call . . . today*. Calphurnia improvizes excuses for Cæsar. What movements or gestures are appropriate to Cæsar's yielding?

56 *for thy humour*, because of your mood of fear.

60 *happy*, apt, favourable.

63 *Cannot . . . falser*. Why does Cæsar add this—to assert his authority, to hide a feeling of shame, to rouse his courage, or to make his reasons precise and clear and so to avoid false accusations?

65 *Shall . . . lie?* Calphurnia's interruption is unfortunate just after Cæsar has assumed the responsibility for the decision. Suddenly Cæsar is roused to assume the public figure, the kindly husband becomes the majestic, uncorruptible public figure.

70 *Lest . . . at*. i.e. with scathing disbelief.

76-9 *She . . . it*. How do Decius and Calphurnia react as Cæsar recounts the dream?

CALPHURNIA: Alas, my lord,
  Your wisdom is consumed in confidence.
  Do not go forth today. Call it my fear   50
  That keeps you in the house, and not your own.
  We'll send Mark Antony to the Senate House,
  And he shall say you are not well today.
  Let me upon my knee prevail in this.
CÆSAR: Mark Antony shall say I am not well,
  And for thy humour I will stay at home.

Enter DECIUS

  Here's Decius Brutus, he shall tell them so.
DECIUS: Cæsar, all hail. Good morrow worthy Cæsar.
  I come to fetch you to the Senate House.
CÆSAR: And you are come in very happy time   60
  To bear my greeting to the senators,
  And tell them that I will not come today.
  Cannot, is false; and that I dare not, falser;
  I will not come today. Tell them so, Decius.
CALPHURNIA: Say he is sick.
CÆSAR: Shall Cæsar send a lie?
  Have I in conquest streched mine arm so far
  To be afeard to tell graybeards the truth?
  Decius, go tell them Cæsar will not come.
DECIUS: Most mighty Cæsar, let me know some cause,
  Lest I be laughed at when I tell them so.   70
CÆSAR: The cause is in my will; I will not come;
  That is enough to satisfy the senate.
  But for your private satisfaction,
  Because I love you, I will let you know.
  Calphurnia here, my wife, stays me at home.
  She dreamt tonight she saw my statue,
  Which like a fountain with an hundred spouts
  Did run pure blood; and many lusty Romans

80   *apply*, interpret.

83–90 *This . . . signified*. How should this be spoken—with firmness, with a genial sweeping aside of Calphurnia's fears, with hesitant phrasing as he makes up the interpretation, anxiously and tensely?

89   *tinctures*, (*a*) honourable additions to coats-of-arms, (*b*) cloths dipped in blood. *stains*, cloths stained with blood. *relics*, i.e. as of a saint. *cognizance*, coats of arms, badges, marks of distinction.

93–4 *the . . . Cæsar*. Emphatic. How do Cæsar and Calphurnia receive this news?

96–7 *a . . . rendered*, the kind of sarcastic remark to be expected.

98–9, '*Break . . . dreams*', '*Lo . . . afraid.*' Mocking imitations of the sup-
101 posed speakers.

100   *hide*. The word insinuates cowardice to Cæsar's action.

102–3 *dear . . . proceeding*. Is this hypocritical, ironic, treacherous?

104   *And . . . liable*, either, my love for you over-rules my discretion or, my reason agrees with my love in this.

107   *robe*. The furred robe worn in Elizabethan times. Who brings his robe and helps him on with it?

Came smiling, and did bathe their hands in it.
And these does she apply for warnings and portents 80
Of evils imminent; and on her knee
Hath begged that I will stay at home today.

DECIUS: This dream is all amiss interpreted;
It was a vision fair and fortunate.
Your statue spouting blood in many pipes,
In which so many smiling Romans bathed,
Signifies that from you great Rome shall suck
Reviving blood, and that great men shall press
For tinctures, stains, relics, and cognizance.
This by Calphurnia's dream is signified. 90

CÆSAR: And this way have you well expounded it.

DECIUS: I have, when you have heard what I can say;
And know it now: the senate have concluded
To give this day a crown to mighty Cæsar.
If you shall send them word you will not come,
Their minds may change. Besides, it were a mock
Apt to be rendered for some one to say,
'Break up the senate till another time,
When Cæsar's wife shall meet with better dreams.'
If Cæsar hide himself, shall they not whisper, 100
'Lo Cæsar is afraid'?
Pardon me Cæsar, for my dear dear love
To your proceeding bids me tell you this;
And reason to my love is liable.

CÆSAR: How foolish do your fears seem now Calphurnia!
I am ashamed I did yield to them.
Give me my robe, for I will go.

Enter BRUTUS, LIGARIUS, METELLUS, CASCA, TREBONIUS, CINNA, *and* PUBLIUS

And look where Publius is come to fetch me.

PUBLIUS: Good morrow Cæsar.

109–   *Welcome ... together.* Cæsar now in good spirits becomes a brisk,
  27   cheerful, affable, courteous host.

110   *What ... too.* Innocently ironic in view of Brutus' sleeplessness.

113   *ague,* fever.

114   *eight.* This confirms the meeting of the conspirators and increases
     the tension.

116   Does the arrival of Antony disconcert the conspirators or not?

118   *prepare within,* i.e. the wine.

122–3 *Remember ... you.* Irony made clear by Trebonius' aside.

125–7 The repetition of 'friends' has an irony which provokes Brutus'
      comment.

127   *like,* (*a*) as if, (*b*) as friends do.

128   *That ... same,* 'like' does not always mean sameness (as in (*b*)
     above); it could mean that being like friends was in fact very
     different from being friends.

129   *yearns,* grieves.

     Brutus is touched with regret. Is this due to his love for Cæsar,
     dislike of deceit, breach in friendship? Is its dramatic value to
     increase respect for Brutus, and so to balance in Brutus Cæsar's
     good natured hospitality, to raise pity for Cæsar, to ensure that the
     audience is in no doubt about the conspirators?

CÆSAR: Welcome Publius.
What, Brutus, are you stirred so early too?   110
Good morrow Casca. Caius Ligarius,
Cæsar was ne'er so much your enemy
As that same ague which hath made you lean.
What is't o'clock?
BRUTUS: Cæsar, 'tis strucken eight.
CÆSAR: I thank you for your pains and courtesy.

Enter ANTONY

See, Antony, that revels long a-nights,
Is notwithstanding up. Good morrow Antony.
ANTONY: So to most noble Cæsar.
CÆSAR: Bid them prepare within.
I am to blame to be thus waited for.
Now Cinna; now, Metellus; what, Trebonius.   120
I have an hour's talk in store for you;
Remember that you call on me today.
Be near me, that I may remember you.
TREBONIUS: Cæsar I will: [*Aside*] and so near will I be,
That your best friends shall wish I had been further.
CÆSAR: Good friends go in, and taste some wine with me;
And we, like friends, will straightway go together.
BRUTUS: [*Aside*] That every like is not the same, O Cæsar,
The heart of Brutus yearns to think upon.   [*Exeunt*

A street

How should Artemidorus enter—boldly, stealthily, furtively, cautiously, timidly, dreamily?

How should he read—quaveringly, intoningly, monotonously, in a high pitch?

6   *look about you*, be on the watch, look out. *Security*, over-confidence. *gives way*, leaves the way open.

7   *lover*, friend.

9   *Here*. Where abouts on the stage?

10   *suitor*, one who asks a favour.

12   *Out . . . emulation*, free from the biting attacks of envy.

14   *Fates*. In classical myth the three goddesses who wove the web of each man's destiny. *contrive*, plot.

Before Brutus' house

Portia's entry and movements should show her feverish restlessness and tension.

4–5   Portia has not thought out what the errand is to be.

6–9   Portia in the stress of her anxiety turns aside from Lucius.

6   *constancy*, self-control.

SCENE THREE

Enter ARTEMIDORUS *reading a paper*

ARTEMIDORUS: 'Cæsar, beware of Brutus; take heed of Cassius;
come not near Casca; have an eye to Cinna; trust not Trebonius; mark well Metellus Cimber; Decius Brutus loves thee
not; thou hast wronged Caius Ligarius. There is but one mind
in all these men, and it is bent against Cæsar. If thou beest not
immortal, look about you. Security gives way to conspiracy.
The mighty gods defend thee. Thy lover,

ARTEMIDORUS.'

Here will I stand till Cæsar pass along,
And as a suitor will I give him this.   10
My heart laments that virtue cannot live
Out of the teeth of emulation.
If thou read this, O Cæsar, thou mayst live;
If not, the Fates with traitors do contrive.   [*Exit*

SCENE FOUR

Enter PORTIA *and* LUCIUS

PORTIA: I prithee boy, run to the Senate House;
Stay not to answer me, but get thee gone.
Why dost thou stay?
LUCIUS: To know my errand madam.
PORTIA: I would have had thee there and here again,
Ere I can tell thee what thou shouldst do there.
O constancy, be strong upon my side,
Set a huge mountain 'tween my heart and tongue.
I have a man's mind, but a woman's might.

9   *How . . . counsel*, i.e. Portia has been told of the plot.

13–15 *Yes . . . him.* What do the short sentences suggest—breathlessness, agitation, make-shift instructions, difficulty in hiding her thoughts?

18   *bustling rumour*, confused noise.

S.D.   *Soothsayer.* An effective heightening of tension as events come to a head in the Capitol, and a further fretting of Portia's overstrained mind.

Portia's agonized alarm increases as she hears the soothsayer's suit until the horrifying, anticipatory 'suitors, Will crowd a feeble man almost to death' breaks down her resistance.

How hard it is for women to keep counsel!
Art thou here yet?

LUCIUS: Madam, what should I do?   10
Run to the Capitol, and nothing else?
And so return to you, and nothing else?

PORTIA: Yes, bring me word boy, if thy lord look well,
For he went sickly forth; and take good note
What Cæsar doth, what suitors press to him.
Hark boy, what noise is that?

LUCIUS: I hear none madam,

PORTIA: Prithee listen well.
I heard a bustling rumour, like a fray,
And the wind brings it from the Capitol.

LUCIUS: Sooth madam, I hear nothing.   20

Enter the SOOTHSAYER

PORTIA: Come hither fellow. Which way hast thou been?

SOOTHSAYER: At mine own house, good lady.

PORTIA: What is't aclock?

SOOTHSAYER: About the ninth hour lady.

PORTIA: Is Cæsar yet gone to the Capitol?

SOOTHSAYER: Madam not yet, I go to take my stand,
To see him pass on to the Capitol.

PORTIA: Thou hast some suit to Cæsar, hast thou not?

SOOTHSAYER: That I have lady, if it will please Cæsar
To be so good to Cæsar as to hear me,
I shall beseech him to befriend himself.

PORTIA: Why, know'st thou any harm's intended towards him?   30

SOOTHSAYER: None that I know will be, much that I fear may
chance.
Good morrow to you. Here the street is narrow.
The throng that follows Cæsar at the heels,
Of senators, of prætors, common suitors,
Will crowd a feeble man almost to death.

39–46   *I . . . thee*. Does Portia speak in a whisper, with a moan, hysterically, with varying speed, pitch and intensity?

40   *heart*, courage, resolution.

41   *speed*, grant success.

44–6   *Run . . . thee*. A flicker of courage. Any gesture or movement? Lucius should be near to receive her orders.

I'll get me to a place more void, and there
Speak to great Cæsar as he comes along.   [*Exit*
PORTIA: I must go in. Ay me, how weak a thing
The heart of woman is! O Brutus,   40
The heavens speed thee in thine enterprise.
Sure the boy heard me. Brutus hath a suit
That Cæsar will not grant. O, I grow faint.
Run Lucius, and commend me to my lord;
Say I am merry. Come to me again,
And bring me word what he doth say to thee.

[*Exeunt severally*

Rome. Before the Capitol

The staging of this scene presents some difficulties. Sisson's suggestion is that the senators are revealed in the discovery space first, then the citizens enter, and finally Cæsar enters. Alternatively the crowd and the procession may come from the yard of the theatre to the stage which represents the Capitol (see Introduction p. 17). When do Artemidorus and the Soothsayer enter? The place of action changes at l. 12.

Is Cæsar's entry a ceremonial one, or is he leaning informally on Brutus' shoulder, or is he surrounded by the conspirators? How does the Soothsayer come to Cæsar's notice?

1   *The . . . come.* Is Cæsar jocular, contemptuous, thoughtful? What dramatic effect is aimed at—reminder to the audience, heightening of tension or irony?

2   *Ay . . . gone.* How does Cæsar receive this—laughingly, derisively, inattentively, indifferently?

3   *schedule,* scroll.

4–5   *Trebonius . . . suit.* Nothing more is heard of this. Possibly Decius seeks to distract Cæsar's attention from Artemidorus' scroll lest it should endanger the conspiracy.

8   *touches us,* is our private concern. *What . . . served.* Is this pompous, public spirited, hypocritical?

10   *What . . . mad?* What action or intonation by Artemidorus causes this reply? *Sirrah, give place.* Any action?

11–12 *What . . . Capitol.* Cassius resourcefully steers Cæsar away.

13   *I . . . thrive.* Is this said—openly, furtively, or casually?

14   *What enterprise Popilius?* How should Cassius say this—sharply, slowly with emphasis on 'enterprise', innocently, chokingly?

15   *What . . . Lena?* What look, gesture or inflection of voice of Cassius drew Brutus' attention?

15–24 *What . . . change.* The sudden alarm and tension can be emphasized by rapid speaking.

18   *makes to,* makes his way towards.

19   *sudden,* quick. *prevention,* anticipation, forestalling.

19–22 *Casca . . . myself.* What is Cassius—excitable, desperate, in a panic, uncontrolled, wild, at a loss, unreliable, hysterical?

ACT THREE

SCENE ONE

A crowd of people; among them ARTEMIDORUS *and the* SOOTH-
SAYER. *Flourish. Enter* CÆSAR, BRUTUS, CASSIUS, CASCA,
DECIUS, METELLUS, TREBONIUS, CINNA, ANTONY,
LEPIDUS, POPILIUS, PUBLIUS, *and others*

CÆSAR: The ides of March are come.

SOOTHSAYER: Ay Cæsar, but not gone.

ARTEMIDORUS: Hail Cæsar. Read this schedule.

DECIUS: Trebonius doth desire you to o'er-read
At your best leisure this his humble suit.

ARTEMIDORUS: O Cæsar, read mine first; for mine's a suit
That touches Cæsar nearer. Read it great Cæsar.

CÆSAR: What touches us ourself shall be last served.

ARTEMIDORUS: Delay not Cæsar, read it instantly.

CÆSAR: What, is the fellow mad?

PUBLIUS: Sirrah, give place.   10

CASSIUS: What, urge you your petitions in the street?
Come to the Capitol.

CÆSAR *and the rest enter the Senate*

POPILIUS: I wish your enterprise today may thrive.

CASSIUS: What enterprise Popilius?

POPILIUS: Fare you well.

BRUTUS: What said Popilius Lena?

CASSIUS: He wished today our enterprise might thrive.
I fear our purpose is discovered.

BRUTUS: Look how he makes to Cæsar. Mark him.

CASSIUS: Casca, be sudden, for we fear prevention.

21-2   *Cassius . . . myself*, i.e. either Cassius or Cæsar will not return alive for (if I do not kill Cæsar) I will kill myself.

22   *be constant*, stand firm, control yourself.

24   *change*, i.e. expression.

28   *presently*, now, at once. *prefer*, lay before, present.

29   *addressed*, ready, prepared. *second*, support.

31   *Are . . . ready?* Apt irony.

      Cæsar . . . senate. Is this arrogance, presumption, pride, formal announcement, egotism, assumption of royalty, or of their unity in administering justice? *redress.* An ironic echo of II. i, 47, 55, 57, 124. What is amiss he is about to redress by his death.

      seat, mightiness, majesty.

      couchings . . . courtesies, grovellings and humble bowings.

37   *fire the blood*, inflate with pride.

38   *And . . . decree*, and reduce what has been ordained and decreed from the beginning.

39   *law.* Johnson's emendation of the Folio's 'lane'. 'lune', freakishness, has also been suggested.

39-40   *fond, To*, so foolish as to.

40   *rebel blood*, unstable character.

41-6   *thawed, melteth, sweet, base spaniel fawning, fawn, cur.* These images are commonly linked by Shakespeare to express contempt for flattery.

42   *melteth*, beguiles, persuades.

43   *low-crooked*, with bended knee. *spaniel fawning*, cringing, wheedling like a spaniel.

46   *spurn*, kick.

47-8   *Know . . . satisfied.* Ben Jonson, Shakespeare's fellow dramatist, stated that Shakespeare had given Cæsar the absurd statement, 'Cæsar did never wrong but with just cause'. If this is so Shakespeare presumably altered the passage to its present form as a result of Jonson's criticism.

Brutus, what shall be done? If this be known,   20
Cassius or Cæsar never shall turn back,
For I will slay myself.

BRUTUS: Cassius be constant.
Popilius Lena speaks not of our purposes,
For look, he smiles, and Cæsar doth not change.

CASSIUS: Trebonius knows his time; for look you Brutus,
He draws Mark Antony out of the way.

[Exeunt Antony and Trebonius

DECIUS: Where is Metellus Cimber? Let him go,
And presently prefer his suit to Cæsar.

BRUTUS: He is addressed; press near and second him.

CINNA: Casca, you are the first that rears your hand.   30

CÆSAR: Are we all ready? What is now amiss
That Cæsar and his senate must redress?

METELLUS: Most high, most mighty, and most puissant Cæsar,
Metellus Cimber throws before thy seat
An humble heart.   *[Kneeling*

CÆSAR: I must prevent thee Cimber.
These couchings, and these lowly courtesies
Might fire the blood of ordinary men,
And turn pre-ordinance and first decree
Into the law of children. Be not fond,
To think that Cæsar bears such rebel blood   40
That will be thawed from the true quality
With that which melteth fools; I mean sweet words,
Low-crooked curtsies, and base spaniel fawning.
Thy brother by decree is banished.
If thou dost bend, and pray, and fawn for him,
I spurn thee like a cur out of my way.
Know, Cæsar doth not wrong, nor without cause
Will he be satisfied.

METELLUS: Is there no voice more worthy than my own,
To sound more sweetly in great Cæsar's ear   50

51 *repealing*, recalling from exile.

52 *I ... hand.* A touch of Judas? *but ... flattery.* In what—humility, sincerity, friendship, love, hypocrisy, flattery?

55 *What, Brutus?* Is this—surprise, dismay, anger, shock?

55-7 *Pardon ... Cimber.* This further piece of slavish fawning diverts attention from Brutus' act of kneeling (l. 75), and the combined exaggerated obsequiousness of these men, Cæsar's friends, provokes Cæsar into angry, overdrawn defence of his integrity.

57 *enfranchisement*, freedom.

58-9 *I ... me*, no doubt I would yield to pleadings if I, like you, could lower myself to beg others to change their views. Cæsar is scornful, i.e. if I could sink to such abject crawling as you are doing, my mind would be as supple as yours, and I would succumb to such blandishments.

60 *northern*, pole.

61 *true-fixed ... quality*, immovable and unchanging.

62 *fellow*, equal.

65 *hold his place*, remain fixed.

67 *apprehensive*, intelligent, reasoning.

69 *unassailable.* Ironic.

70 *Unshaked of motion*, undisturbed, unyielding to pleadings, immovable. Perhaps 'motion' is a glance back at 'move' ll. 58-9, and an ironic echo of I. ii, 315-16.

Is Cæsar's comparison of himself with the pole-star—ironic, arrogant, boastful, bombastic, hyperbolical, ominous, a recalling to the audience of the disorder in the heavens, a challenge to the gods?

74 *Wilt ... Olympus*, will you try the impossible? *Olympus.* The mountain in Thessaly reputed to be the home of the gods. The word suggests that Cæsar is god-like.

75 *bootless*, vainly.

76 *Speak ... me!* During Cæsar's speech how have the conspirators grouped themselves? How has Casca got in position?

77 *Et tu Brute?* Is this—a shout of anguish, a reproach, a prophecy, a horrified recognition of his friend's treachery, a moment of bitter truth? *Then fall Cæsar!* After Cæsar saw Brutus among the conspirators it is said that he muffled his face in his robe and ceased to defend himself. For the stage action involved in the murder bear in mind l. 115.

How do the senators and citizens behave, are they—silent, apathetic, restless, confused, noisy, stampeding? (See ll. 82-3.)

For the repealing of my banished brother?

BRUTUS: I kiss thy hand, but not in flattery Cæsar;
Desiring thee that Publius Cimber may
Have an immediate freedom of repeal.

CÆSAR: What, Brutus?

CASSIUS:　　　　　　　Pardon Cæsar; Cæsar, pardon:
As low as to thy foot doth Cassius fall,
To beg enfranchisement for Publius Cimber.

CÆSAR: I could be well moved, if I were as you;
If I could pray to move, prayers would move me.
But I am constant as the northern star,　　　　　　　60
Of whose true-fixed and resting quality
There is no fellow in the firmament.
The skies are painted with unnumbered sparks,
They are all fire, and every one doth shine;
But there's but one in all doth hold his place.
So in the world; 'tis furnished well with men,
And men are flesh and blood, and apprehensive;
Yet in the number I do know but one
That unassailable holds on his rank,
Unshaked of motion; and that I am he,　　　　　　　70
Let me a little show it, even in this,
That I was constant Cimber should be banished,
And constant do remain to keep him so.

CINNA: O Cæsar—

CÆSAR:　　　　　　Hence! Wilt thou lift up Olympus?

DECIUS: Great Cæsar—

CÆSAR:　　　　　　Doth not Brutus bootless kneel?

CASCA: Speak hands for me!　　　　　[*They stab Cæsar*

CÆSAR: Et tu Brute? Then fall Cæsar!　　　　[*Dies*

78   *Liberty . . . dead.* A tremendous shout of triumph.

80   *common pulpits*, public platforms.

83   *Ambition's . . . paid*, i.e. Cæsar has received the reward of his ambition.

84   *to the pulpit*, i.e. to reassure the people.

85   *Publius*, an aged senator. Is Brutus considerate or astute in singling out Publius?

86   *confounded*, bewildered. *mutiny*, uproar.

89   *Talk . . . standing*, there is no need to stand on the defensive. *good cheer*, be at ease.

93   *mischief*, injury.

94   *abide*, pay for, bear the consequences of.

96   *amazed*, utterly astounded.

98   *Fates.* In classical myth the three goddesses who wove a cloth representing each man's destiny.

100   *drawing days out*, prolonging of life. *stand upon*, consider important.

101–2   *Why . . . death.* Is this a jest, a serious thought, or just Casca?

105–10   *Stoop . . . liberty!* This episode is Shakespeare's invention. What dramatic purpose has it—an ironic prelude to the cry 'Peace', a symbolical acceptance of responsibility by the conspirators, a savage, horrifying spectacle to excite the spectators, a fulfilment of Calphurnia's prophetic dream, a revelation of the bloodthirstiness of the murderers and the degeneration of Brutus' character?

CINNA: Liberty! Freedom! Tyranny is dead.
    Run hence, proclaim, cry it about the streets.
CASSIUS: Some to the common pulpits, and cry out,   80
    'Liberty, freedom, and enfranchisement!'
BRUTUS: People and senators, be not affrighted.
    Fly not, stand still. Ambition's debt is paid.
CASCA: Go to the pulpit Brutus.
DECIUS: And Cassius too.
BRUTUS: Where's Publius?
CINNA: Here, quite confounded with this mutiny.
METELLUS: Stand fast together, lest some friend of Cæsar's
    Should chance—
BRUTUS: Talk not of standing. Publius, good cheer;
    There is no harm intended to your person,   90
    Nor to no Roman else. So tell them Publius.
CASSIUS: And leave us Publius, lest that the people
    Rushing on us should do your age some mischief.
BRUTUS: Do so; and let no man abide this deed,
    But we the doers.

Enter TREBONIUS

CASSIUS: Where is Antony?
TREBONIUS: Fled to his house amazed.
    Men, wives, and children stare, cry out, and run,
    As it were doomsday.
BRUTUS: Fates, we will know your pleasures.
    That we shall die we know; 'tis but the time,
    And drawing days out, that men stand upon.   100
CASCA: Why he that cuts off twenty years of life
    Cuts off so many years of fearing death.
BRUTUS: Grant that, and then is death a benefit;
    So are we Cæsar's friends, that have abridged
    His time of fearing death. Stoop Romans, stoop,
    And let us bathe our hands in Cæsar's blood

111– *How . . . liberty*, i.e. we are assured of immortal fame. A challenge
  18   to destiny which the intruding topical reference to this play in
       particular underlines with irony.

112   *lofty scene*, sublime action, mighty deed.

114   *in sport*, in a play.

115   *Pompey's basis*, the base of Pompey's statue.

117   *knot*, group (of conspirators). Possibly a quibble with 'liberty', i.e.
       the 'knot' (tie) that, contrary to its normal usage, released the
       country.

122   *Soft . . . Antony's.* This quiet entry of a single servant is held by
       some to be a turning point in the play.
            His entry changes the intentions of the conspirators. Are they
       alarmed, tense, curious or disconcerted?

123–5 *Thus . . . say.* Some see in this elaborate bowing a mocking parody
       of the conspirators' kneeling before Cæsar. Is the servant also very
       much afraid?

126   *honest*, honourable.

130   *vouchsafe*, graciously permit.

131   *resolved*, satisfied.

136   *untrod state*, unknown state of things.

Up to the elbows, and besmear our swords;
Then walk we forth, even to the market place,
And waving our red weapons o'er our heads,
Let's all cry, 'Peace, freedom, and liberty!'   110
CASSIUS: Stoop then, and wash. How many ages hence
  Shall this our lofty scene be acted over,
  In states unborn and accents yet unknown.
BRUTUS: How many times shall Cæsar bleed in sport,
  That now on Pompey's basis lies along,
  No worthier than the dust.
CASSIUS: So oft as that shall be,
  So often shall the knot of us be called
  The men that gave their country liberty.
DECIUS: What, shall we forth?
CASSIUS: Ay, every man away.
  Brutus shall lead, and we will grace his heels   120
  With the most boldest and best hearts of Rome.

Enter a SERVANT

BRUTUS: Soft, who comes here? A friend of Antony's.
SERVANT: Thus Brutus, did my master bid me kneel;
  Thus did Mark Antony bid me fall down,
  And being prostrate thus he bade me say:
  Brutus is noble, wise, valiant, and honest;
  Cæsar was mighty, bold, royal, and loving.
  Say I love Brutus, and I honour him;
  Say I feared Cæsar, honoured him, and loved him.
  If Brutus will vouchsafe that Antony   130
  May safely come to him, and be resolved
  How Cæsar hath deserved to lie in death,
  Mark Antony shall not love Cæsar dead
  So well as Brutus living; but will follow
  The fortunes and affairs of noble Brutus
  Through the hazards of this untrod state

142   *presently*, immediately.

143   *well to friend*, a good friend.

144–5 *yet . . . much*, yet a great fear of him is in my mind.

145–6 *my . . . purpose*, my misgivings always turn out to be unpleasantly
close to the truth (Arden).

147   Antony's entry should be significant. Is it slow, thoughtful, brisk,
or dignified? Does he ignore Brutus' welcome through the shock
of seeing Cæsar's body, or does he salute Brutus with a silent
gesture?

152   *be let blood*, (*a*) be killed, (*b*) be bled to improve health. See II. i,
180. *rank*, (*a*) diseased for which the cure was to be bled, (*b*)
overgrown and to be cut down.

157   *bear me hard*, have hard feelings against me.

158   *purpled*, crimsoned.

159   *Fulfil your pleasure*, complete what it has pleased you to begin.

161   *mean of death*, way of dying.

     Antony, assured of his safety by Brutus, challenges the con-
spirators to kill him. Why—to taunt them, to embarrass them, to
prove his courage, to put them in an inferior position by taking
the lead, so that they now become suitors to him?

With all true faith. So says my master Antony.

BRUTUS: Thy master is a wise and valiant Roman;
I never thought him worse.
Tell him, so please him come unto this place,   140
He shall be satisfied; and by my honour
Depart untouched.

SERVANT: I'll fetch him presently.   [*Exit*

BRUTUS: I know that we shall have him well to friend.

CASSIUS: I wish we may. But yet have I a mind
That fears him much; and my misgiving still
Falls shrewdly to the purpose.

BRUTUS: But here comes Antony.

Enter ANTONY

                        Welcome Mark Antony.

ANTONY: O mighty Cæsar! Dost thou lie so low?
Are all thy conquests, glories, triumphs, spoils,
Shrunk to this little measure? Fare thee well.   150
I know not gentlemen what you intend,
Who else must be let blood, who else is rank;
If I myself, there is no hour so fit
As Cæsar's death hour, nor no instrument
Of half that worth as those your swords, made rich
With the most noble blood of all this world.
I do beseech ye, if you bear me hard,
Now, whilst your purpled hands do reek and smoke,
Fulfil your pleasure. Live a thousand years,
I shall not find myself so apt to die;   160
No place will please me so, no mean of death,
As here by Cæsar, and by you cut off,
The choice and master spirits of this age.

BRUTUS: O Antony, beg not your death of us.
Though now we must appear bloody and cruel,
As by our hands and this our present act,

171   *As . . . fire*. Proverbial. *so pity pity*, so pity (for the wrongs suffered by Rome) has driven out pity (for Cæsar).

173   *swords . . . points*, swords have no harmful purpose. Such swords were used in practice.

174   *Our . . . malice*. Many other words have been proposed for 'malice'. Of these 'amity' has received some support.

       The conspirators' arms, however, are steeped in blood and the contrast between 'arms' and 'hearts' parallels the similar contrast in ll. 166–9.

175   *temper*, harmony, disposition.

177–8   *Your . . . dignities*. To what is Cassius appealing—Antony's ambition, materialism, comradeship?

177   *voice*, vote, authority.

178   *disposing . . . dignities*, granting of honours or appointments to important posts.

179–   *Only . . . proceeded*. Brutus is already on the defensive and almost
83   apologetic in stressing his love for Cæsar and asking Antony to be patient.

183   *I . . . wisdom*. Perhaps ironic.

184   *Let . . . hand*. This elaborate handshaking echoes Brutus' hand-shaking (II. i, 112). Are the conspirators glad, embarrassed or reluctant to shake hands?

188   *valiant Casca*. A touch of irony.

191   *credit*, reputation. *slippery ground*. It has been suggested that this is a side-reference to Cæsar's blood on the ground (Arden).

192   *conceit*, think of, regard.

194–   *That . . . lethe*. Does this appeal to the dead Cæsar spring from
206   love for Cæsar, shame at his own action, desire to test the mood of the conspirators?

You see we do; yet see you but our hands,
And this the bleeding business they have done.
Our hearts you see not, they are pitiful;
And pity to the general wrong of Rome—   170
As fire drives out fire, so pity pity—
Hath done this deed on Cæsar. For your part,
To you our swords have leaden points, Mark Antony;
Our arms, in strength of malice, and our hearts
Of brothers' temper, do receive you in
With all kind love, good thoughts, and reverence.

CASSIUS: Your voice shall be as strong as any man's
In the disposing of new dignities.

BRUTUS: Only be patient till we have appeased
The multitude, beside themselves with fear,   180
And then we will deliver you the cause,
Why I, that did love Cæsar when I struck him,
Have thus proceeded.

ANTONY: I doubt not of your wisdom.
Let each man render me his bloody hand.
First Marcus Brutus, will I shake with you;
Next Caius Cassius, do I take your hand;
Now Decius Brutus yours; now yours Metellus;
Yours Cinna; and my valiant Casca, yours;
Though last, not least in love, yours good Trebonius.
Gentlemen all—alas, what shall I say?   190
My credit now stands on such slippery ground,
That one of two bad ways you must conceit me,
Either a coward or a flatterer.
That I did love thee Cæsar, O 'tis true.
If then thy spirit look upon us now,
Shall it not grieve thee dearer than thy death,
To see thy Antony making his peace,
Shaking the bloody fingers of thy foes,
Most noble, in the presence of thy corse?

202   *close*, agree, join.

204   *bayed*, hunted to a standstill. *hart*, (*a*) deer, (*b*) heart.

206   *Signed . . . spoil*, bearing on them the marks of thy slaughter. Those hunters in at the death were marked with the blood of the dead deer. See II. i, 174. *spoil*, the killing of the hunted animal and the distribution of its parts to the hounds. See II. i, 174. *lethe*, (*a*) death, (*b*) life-blood whose flowing brings the forgetfulness of death. Lethe in classical myth was a river in Hades. The drinking of its waters brought forgetfulness.

207   *forest . . . hart*, i.e. its natural kingdom.

212–   *The . . . modesty*. Is this a quick excuse to disarm Cassius' sus-
13   picions, or a retort putting Cassius in his place?

213   *cold modesty*, small measure of praise.

216   *pricked*, marked on the list.

224   *regard*, considerations.

227–30 *suitor . . . funeral*. The most important matter slipped in casually.

230   *order . . . funeral*, ceremony of his funeral.

Had I as many eyes as thou hast wounds, 200
Weeping as fast as they stream forth thy blood,
It would become me better than to close
In terms of friendship with thine enemies.
Pardon me Julius! Here wast thou bayed, brave hart;
Here didst thou fall; and here thy hunters stand,
Signed in thy spoil, and crimsoned in thy lethe.
O world, thou wast the forest to this hart,
And this, indeed, O world, the heart of thee.
How like a deer, strucken by many princes,
Dost thou here lie. 210

CASSIUS: Mark Antony—

ANTONY: Pardon me Caius Cassius,
The enemies of Cæsar shall say this;
Then, in a friend, it is cold modesty.

CASSIUS: I blame you not for praising Cæsar so,
But what compact mean you to have with us?
Will you be pricked in number of our friends,
Or shall we on, and not depend on you?

ANTONY: Therefore I took your hands, but was indeed
Swayed from the point by looking down on Cæsar.
Friends am I with you all, and love you all, 220
Upon this hope, that you shall give me reasons
Why, and wherein, Cæsar was dangerous.

BRUTUS: Or else were this a savage spectacle.
Our reasons are so full of good regard,
That were you, Antony, the son of Cæsar,
You should be satisfied.

ANTONY: That's all I seek;
And am moreover suitor that I may
Produce his body to the market place,
And in the pulpit, as becomes a friend,
Speak in the order of his funeral. 230

BRUTUS: You shall, Mark Antony.

235– *By . . . wrong*. Again Brutus over-rules Cassius and commits a
42   second mistake.

237   *our Cæsar's*. A familiar, almost affectionate phrase, as if all of them
      killed Cæsar with regret.
238   *protest*, announce, proclaim.
      Is Brutus' suggestion—stupid, naive, generous, noble, fatuous,
      pathetic, incredible?

243   *fall*, happen.

246   *devise*, think out.

254–75 During this speech does Antony kneel, stand, move, gesture?
255   *butchers*. Emphatic—an echo of II. i, 166.
256   *ruins*, remains.
257   *tide of times*, stream of time.

260   *dumb mouths*. See III. ii, 222. For the association of 'wounds' and
      'mouths'. See *1 Henry IV*, I. iii, 97; *Richard III*, I. ii, 56.

CASSIUS: Brutus, a word with you.
  [*Aside to Brutus*] You know not what you do. Do not consent
  That Antony speak in his funeral.
  Know you how much the people may be moved
  By that which he will utter?
BRUTUS: By your pardon;
  I will myself into the pulpit first,
  And show the reason of our Cæsar's death.
  What Antony shall speak, I will protest
  He speaks by leave, and by permission;
  And that we are contented Cæsar shall   240
  Have all true rites, and lawful ceremonies.
  It shall advantage more than do us wrong.
CASSIUS: I know not what may fall; I like it not.
BRUTUS: Mark Antony, here take you Cæsar's body.
  You shall not in your funeral speech blame us,
  But speak all good you can devise of Cæsar,
  And say you do't by our permission;
  Else shall you not have any hand at all
  About his funeral. And you shall speak
  In the same pulpit whereto I am going,   250
  After my speech is ended.
ANTONY: Be it so;
  I do desire no more.
BRUTUS: Prepare the body then, and follow us.
                              [*Exeunt all but Antony*
ANTONY: O pardon me, thou bleeding piece of earth,
  That I am meek and gentle with these butchers.
  Thou art the ruins of the noblest man
  That ever lived in the tide of times.
  Woe to the hand that shed this costly blood!
  Over thy wounds now do I prophesy,
  Which like dumb mouths do ope their ruby lips,   260
  To beg the voice and utterance of my tongue,

262 ff How can this be made effective—by pitch of voice, speed, gesture or posture?

262 *limbs*, i.e. bodies.

264 *cumber*, harass.

265 *in use*, common, customary.

268 *quartered*, cut in pieces.

269 *All . . . deeds*, all feelings of pity shall be deadened by familiarity with bloodthirsty deeds.

270 *ranging*, roving in search of prey.

271 *Ate*. In classical myth the goddess of mischief and destruction.

273 *Cry havoc*. The order for pillage and slaughter of the defeated given by monarchs only. *let . . . war*. Possibly famine, slaughter and fire. See *Henry V*, Prol. 7. *slip*, the technical word for releasing a hound quickly to pursue its prey.

274 *foul*, (*a*) evil, (*b*) stinking.

275 *carrion*, corpse-like.

281 *O Cæsar!* As he catches sight of Cæsar's body.

282 *big*, swollen with grief.

283 *Passion*, grief, sorrow.

287 *Post*, ride, travel.

289 *Rome*, (*a*) Rome, (*b*) room. See I. ii, 156.

290 *Hie*, hurry.

292, 284 *try, issue*. Legal terms. *try*, judge, test.

A curse shall light upon the limbs of men;
Domestic fury, and fierce civil strife
Shall cumber all the parts of Italy;
Blood and destruction shall be so in use,
And dreadful objects so familiar,
That mothers shall but smile when they behold
Their infants quartered with the hands of war;
All pity choked with custom of fell deeds;
And Cæsar's spirit ranging for revenge,   270
With Ate by his side come hot from hell,
Shall in these confines with a monarch's voice
Cry havoc, and let slip the dogs of war,
That this foul deed shall smell above the earth
With carrion men, groaning for burial.

Enter a SERVANT

You serve Octavius Cæsar, do you not?
SERVANT: I do Mark Antony.
ANTONY: Cæsar did write for him to come to Rome.
SERVANT: He did receive his letters, and is coming,
  And bid me say to you by word of mouth—   280
  O Cæsar!
ANTONY: Thy heart is big; get thee apart and weep.
  Passion I see is catching, for mine eyes,
  Seeing those beads of sorrow stand in thine,
  Began to water. Is thy master coming?
SERVANT: He lies tonight within seven leagues of Rome.
ANTONY: Post back with speed, and tell him what hath chanced.
  Here is a mourning Rome, a dangerous Rome,
  No Rome of safety for Octavius yet;
  Hie hence, and tell him so. Yet stay awhile,   290
  Thou shalt not back till I have borne this corse
  Into the market place. There shall I try
  In my oration, how the people take

294   *issue*, (*a*) i.e. of blood, (*b*) result of the cruelty, (*c*) matter to be decided.

297   *Lend . . . hand.* Why? Is Antony grief stricken, exhausted mourning or kneeling?

The Forum

How do the citizens enter—riotously, clamorously, threateningly, fiercely?

4   *part*, split up, divide.

7   *public reasons*, i.e. why Cæsar's murder was for the public good. Brutus ascends the pulpit while the citizens are speaking.

9–10   *I . . . rendered.* Is the citizen suspicious, threatening, aggressive, canny?

10   *severally*, separately.
        The use of prose for Brutus' speech emphasizes its lack of emotional appeal.

13–17   *hear . . . judge.* Notice the emphatic positioning of the repeated words; in the last sentence it is the thought that is repeated.

15   *Censure*, judge.

16   *senses*, understanding.

20–1   *not . . . more.* Brutus effectively summarizes his 'cause' in balanced opposing phrases.

The cruel issue of these bloody men;
According to the which, thou shalt discourse
To young Octavius of the state of things.
Lend me your hand.   [*Exeunt with Cæsar's body*

SCENE TWO

Enter BRUTUS *and* CASSIUS, *and* Citizens

CITIZENS: We will be satisfied; let us be satisfied.
BRUTUS: Then follow me, and give me audience, friends.
   Cassius, go you into the other street,
   And part the numbers.
   Those that will hear me speak, let 'em stay here;
   Those that will follow Cassius, go with him;
   And public reasons shall be rendered
   Of Cæsar's death.
FIRST CITIZEN: I will hear Brutus speak.
SECOND CITIZEN: I will hear Cassius, and compare their
      reasons,
   When severally we hear them rendered.   10
                    [*Exit Cassius, with some of the Citizens.*
                       Brutus goes into the pulpit
THIRD CITIZEN: The noble Brutus is ascended. Silence!
BRUTUS: Be patient till the last.
   Romans, countrymen, and lovers, hear me for my cause, and
   be silent, that you may hear. Believe me for mine honour, and
   have respect to mine honour, that you may believe. Censure
   me in your wisdom, and awake your senses, that you may the
   better judge. If there be any in this assembly, any dear friend
   of Cæsar's, to him I say, that Brutus' love to Cæsar was no
   less than his. If then that friend demand why Brutus rose
   against Cæsar, this is my answer—not that I loved Cæsar

21-3 *Had . . . men.* Again the sharp balanced opposition of 'were living
—die— all slaves' and 'were dead—live—all free men'.

25-7 *There . . . ambition.* Brutus repeats his climax in concentrated
form.

27-31 *Who . . . reply.* Brutus' questions stressed by alliteration are cast in
a form that makes impossible a direct answer without self condemnation.

Here are two opinions of Brutus' speech. 'the imitation of the
Attic style as the Roman orators practised it is so perfect that unless
we knew it was Shakespeare's, we might suppose it was a translation'. 'It is one of the worst speeches ever made by an able and
intelligent man. Its symmetrical structure, its balanced sentences,
its ordered procedure, its rhetorical questions . . . its hopelessly
abstract subject matter . . . are the utterance of a man whose heart
is not in his words. It is a dishonest speech'. (See Introduction
pp. 25-6.)

28 *rude,* barbarous, boorish.

34-5 *The . . . Capitol,* the matters that made his death essential are
officially recorded in the Capitol. Possibly Shakespeare had in
mind the official records deposited in the Tower of London
(Wilson).

35 *extenuated,* lessened, diminished.

36 *enforced,* exaggerated, over-stressed.

s.d. *Enter . . . body.* A solemn entry perhaps with muffled drums.

40 *place . . . commonwealth,* i.e. in a free commonwealth now that
Cæsar is dead.

47-8 *Let . . . Brutus.* An ironic comment on the effectiveness of Brutus'
speech and the mentality of the crowd.

less, but that I loved Rome more. Had you rather Cæsar were living, and die all slaves, than that Cæsar were dead, to live all free men? As Cæsar loved me, I weep for him; as he was fortunate, I rejoice at it; as he was valiant, I honour him; but as he was ambitious, I slew him. There is tears, for his love; joy, for his fortune; honour, for his valour; and death, for his ambition. Who is here so base, that would be a bondman? If any, speak, for him have I offended. Who is here so rude that would not be a Roman? If any, speak, for him have I offended. Who is here so vile that will not love his country? If any, speak, for him have I offended. I pause for a reply. 31

ALL: None Brutus, none.

BRUTUS: Then none have I offended. I have done no more to Cæsar than you shall do to Brutus. The question of his death is enrolled in the Capitol; his glory not extenuated, wherein he was worthy; nor his offences enforced, for which he suffered death.

Enter ANTONY *with* CÆSAR'S *body*

Here comes his body, mourned by Mark Antony, who though he had no hand in his death, shall receive the benefit of his dying, a place in the commonwealth, as which of you shall not? With this I depart, that as I slew my best lover for the good of Rome, I have the same dagger for myself, when it shall please my country to need my death. 43

ALL: Live Brutus, live, live!

FIRST CITIZEN: Bring him with triumph home unto his house.

SECOND CITIZEN: Give him a statue with his ancestors.

THIRD CITIZEN: Let him be Cæsar.

FOURTH CITIZEN: Cæsar's better parts
Shall be crowned in Brutus.

FIRST CITIZEN: We'll bring him to his house with shouts and clamours.

BRUTUS: My countrymen—

54 *Do grace*, pay honour. *grace*, respectful attention.
55 *Tending to*, concerning.
        Do some of the crowd see Brutus off the stage or does he depart in isolation?

62 *beholding*, obliged, indebted.

63 *What . . . Brutus?* Is the speaker deaf, suspicious, or threatening?

65–8 '*Twere . . . say.* The remarks indicate the crowd's opinion and its disturbed noisiness.

69 *gentle.* Is this tentative, flattering, ironical, or sincere?

72–3 *The . . . bones.* This bitter proverb apparently accepting the condemnation of Cæsar quietly implies that Cæsar did some good things, and that proverbially it is envy that slanders the dead.
        Having apparently accepted Brutus' statement of Cæsar's ambition, Antony proceeds to undermine it by descriptions of Cæsar's deeds and actions which are in contrast with it.
77 *answered it*, paid for it.

SECOND CITIZEN: Peace, silence, Brutus speaks.   50
FIRST CITIZEN: Peace ho!
BRUTUS: Good countrymen, let me depart alone,
   And, for my sake, stay here with Antony.
   Do grace to Cæsar's corpse, and grace his speech
   Tending to Cæsar's glories, which Mark Antony,
   By our permission, is allowed to make.
   I do entreat you, not a man depart,
   Save I alone, till Antony have spoke.   [*Exit*
FIRST CITIZEN: Stay ho, and let us hear Mark Antony.
THIRD CITIZEN: Let him go up into the public chair.   60
   We'll hear him. Noble Antony go up.
ANTONY: For Brutus' sake, I am beholding to you.
                              [*Goes into the pulpit*
FOURTH CITIZEN: What does he say of Brutus?
THIRD CITIZEN: He says, for Brutus' sake
   He finds himself beholding to us all.
FOURTH CITIZEN: 'Twere best he speak no harm of Brutus
   here.
FIRST CITIZEN: This Cæsar was a tyrant.
THIRD CITIZEN: Nay that's certain.
   We are blest that Rome is rid of him.
SECOND CITIZEN: Peace, let us hear what Antony can say.
ANTONY: You gentle Romans—
CITIZENS: Peace ho, let us hear him.
ANTONY: Friends, Romans, countrymen, lend me your ears:
   I come to bury Cæsar, not to praise him.   71
   The evil that men do lives after them,
   The good is oft interred with their bones;
   So let it be with Cæsar. The noble Brutus
   Hath told you Cæsar was ambitious;
   If it were so, it was a grievous fault,
   And grievously hath Cæsar answered it.
   Here, under leave of Brutus and the rest—

92   *on*, i.e. on the feast of.

101-4   *O . . . me*. Like Brutus ll. 15-17 Antony appeals to judgement but
        introduces at the same time a powerful appeal to emotions.
101   *judgement*, reason. Even beasts who lack reason would show suffi-
        cient judgement to mourn. (See *Hamlet*, I. ii, 150-1.)
105-   *Methinks . . . Antony*. The remarks of the citizens show them to be
    13 affected by his appeal to their reason and their emotions, and by
        his nobility.

108   *I . . . place*. A proverbial expression to the effect that all change is
        for the worse.

For Brutus is an honourable man,
So are they all, all honourable men—   80
Come I to speak in Cæsar's funeral.
He was my friend, faithful and just to me;
But Brutus says he was ambitious,
And Brutus is an honourable man.
He hath brought many captives home to Rome,
Whose ransoms did the general coffers fill.
Did this in Cæsar seem ambitious?
When that the poor have cried, Cæsar hath wept;
Ambition should be made of sterner stuff;
Yet Brutus says he was ambitious,   90
And Brutus is an honourable man.
You all did see that on the Lupercal
I thrice presented him a kingly crown,
Which he did thrice refuse. Was this ambition?
Yet Brutus says he was ambitious,
And sure he is an honourable man.
I speak not to disprove what Brutus spoke,
But here I am to speak what I do know.
You all did love him once, not without cause;
What cause withholds you then to mourn for him?   100
O judgement, thou art fled to brutish beasts,
And men have lost their reason. Bear with me;
My heart is in the coffin there with Cæsar,
And I must pause till it come back to me.

FIRST CITIZEN: Methinks there is much reason in his sayings.
SECOND CITIZEN: If thou consider rightly of the matter,
    Cæsar has had great wrong.
THIRD CITIZEN: Has he masters?
    I fear there will a worse come in his place.
FOURTH CITIZEN: Marked ye his words? He would not take
    the crown;
    Therefore 'tis certain he was not ambitious.   110

111 *dear abide it*, pay dearly for it.

112 *Poor . . . weeping*. Wilson thinks this should be spoken by a
woman.

116 *stood against*, was supreme, defied.

117 *And . . . reverence*, i.e. lower than the meanest man who is therefore superior to him.

119 *mutiny*, riot. An ominous hint.

120-4 *I . . . men*. The issue is now openly put to the citizens.

126 *closet*, study, room.

127-8 *Let . . . read*. This withholding of information followed by a
description of the ecstasy of gratitude such information would
inspire in them rouses the citizens.

129-   *And . . . issue*. Are these the Romans that fulfil Decius' interpreta-
34   tion of Calphurnia's dream, II. ii, 86-90?

130 *napkins*, handkerchiefs, i.e. like the relics and tokens of martyrs.

132-4 *mention . . . issue*. Antony keeps the idea of the 'will' in the minds
of the citizens.

138 *meet*, fitting, right.

138-   *It . . . it*. Antony expresses a tenderness and solicitude for the
43   well-being of the citizens, which, with his apparent slip in mentioning a term of the will, inflames them to fury.

139 *You . . . men*. A better approach than that of Marullus I. i, 37.

140 *will*. From here to l. 155 the word 'will' recurs like a bell.

FIRST CITIZEN: If it be found so, some will dear abide it.

SECOND CITIZEN: Poor soul, his eyes are red as fire with weeping.

THIRD CITIZEN: There's not a nobler man in Rome than Antony.

FOURTH CITIZEN: Now mark him, he begins again to speak,

ANTONY: But yesterday the word of Cæsar might
Have stood against the world; now lies he there,
And none so poor to do him reverence.
O masters, if I were disposed to stir
Your hearts and minds to mutiny and rage,
I should do Brutus wrong, and Cassius wrong,   120
Who you all know are honourable men.
I will not do them wrong; I rather choose
To wrong the dead, to wrong myself and you,
Than I will wrong such honourable men.
But here's a parchment with the seal of Cæsar;
I found it in his closet; 'tis his will.
Let but the commons hear this testament—
Which, pardon me, I do not mean to read—
And they would go and kiss dead Cæsar's wounds,
And dip their napkins in his sacred blood,   130
Yea, beg a hair of him for memory,
And dying, mention it within their wills,
Bequeathing it as a rich legacy
Unto their issue.

FOURTH CITIZEN: We'll hear the will. Read it Mark Antony.

ALL: The will, the will! We will hear Cæsar's will.

ANTONY: Have patience gentle friends, I must not read it.
It is not meet you know how Cæsar loved you.
You are not wood, you are not stones, but men;
And being men, hearing the will of Cæsar,   140
It will inflame you, it will make you mad.
'Tis good you know not that you are his heirs;

147   *O'ershot myself*, gone beyond what I intended.

148-9 *I . . . it.* The bitter irony is vividly pointed by the harsh 'daggers have stabbed Cæsar'.

       Is Antony hypocritical, sarcastic, pious, sorrowful or apologetic?

150   *Honourable men!* How can the scorn and derision be brought out?

155- The numerous stage directions within the text set the scene and
65   the turbulence of the crowd.

164   *Nay . . . off.* A traditional stage practice makes Antony object to the stench of the crowd. Do you agree? *far*, farther.

166 ff Antony holds back the will, he now sets out to invite pity and rage.

167- *I . . . Nervii.* The defeat of the Nervii in Gaul was one of Cæsar's
70   greatest victories, and it was celebrated with unusual magnificence in Rome. Antony was not present. What dramatic value has this reminiscence?

172   *envious*, venomous, malicious.

173   *well-beloved.* Antony stresses Cæsar's love for Brutus. Brutus disregards it in mentioning repeatedly his own love for Cæsar. Is it to emphasize his own self-sacrifice, to avoid admitting his treachery to a friend, or to present Cæsar as remote and tyrannical?

176   *to be resolved*, to make certain.

For if you should, O what would come of it!

FOURTH CITIZEN: Read the will. We'll hear it Antony.
You shall read us the will, Cæsar's will.

ANTONY: Will you be patient? Will you stay awhile?
I have o'ershot myself to tell you of it.
I fear I wrong the honourable men
Whose daggers have stabbed Cæsar; I do fear it.

FOURTH CITIZEN: They were traitors. Honourable men!   150

ALL: The will! The testament!

SECOND CITIZEN: They were villains, murderers. The will,
read the will.

ANTONY: You will compel me then to read the will?
Then make a ring about the corpse of Cæsar,
And let me show you him that made the will.
Shall I descend? And will you give me leave?

ALL: Come down.

SECOND CITIZEN: Descend.

THIRD CITIZEN: You shall have leave.   [*Antony comes down*

FOURTH CITIZEN: A ring, stand round.   161

FIRST CITIZEN: Stand from the hearse, stand from the body.

SECOND CITIZEN: Room for Antony, most noble Antony.

ANTONY: Nay, press not so upon me; stand far off.

SEVERAL CITIZENS: Stand back; room; bear back.

ANTONY: If you have tears, prepare to shed them now.
You all do know this mantle. I remember
The first time ever Cæsar put it on;
'Twas on a summer's evening in his tent,
That day he overcame the Nervii.   170
Look, in this place ran Cassius' dagger through.
See what a rent the envious Casca made.
Through this the well-beloved Brutus stabbed;
And as he plucked his cursed steel away,
Mark how the blood of Cæsar followed it,
As rushing out of doors, to be resolved

177 *unkindly*, (*a*) unnaturally, (*b*) cruelly.

178 *angel*, darling or perhaps guardian spirit.

180 *most unkindest*, (*a*) most unnatural, (*b*) cruellest. Emphatic double superlative.

183 *burst*̈ *. . . heart*, i.e. with grief.

186 *Which . . . blood*. Perhaps out of sympathy, or, at the presence of Cæsar who brought about Pompey's death. It was believed that the body of a murdered man would bleed in the presence of the murderer.

189 *flourished*, (*a*) prospered, was triumphant, (*b*) brandished as a sword. See II. i, 106.

191 *dint*, touch, force.

193–4 *Look . . . traitors*. A sudden, dramatic unveiling, the climax of his speech.
      How do the citizens respond in movement and gesture?

194 *marred*, mutilated.

207–8 *let . . . mutiny*. An appeal that deliberately encourages disorder.

210 *private griefs*. A suggestion that Cæsar's murderers had personal grudges against him. *griefs*, grievances.

If Brutus so unkindly knocked or no;
For Brutus, as you know, was Cæsar's angel.
Judge, O you gods, how dearly Cæsar loved him.
This was the most unkindest cut of all;   180
For when the noble Cæsar saw him stab,
Ingratitude, more strong than traitors' arms,
Quite vanquished him. Then burst his mighty heart;
And in his mantle muffling up his face,
Even at the base of Pompey's statue,
Which all the while ran blood, great Cæsar fell.
O what a fall was there, my countrymen!
Then I, and you, and all of us fell down,
Whilst bloody treason flourished over us.
O now you weep, and I perceive you feel   190
The dint of pity. These are gracious drops.
Kind souls, what weep you when you but behold
Our Cæsar's vesture wounded? Look you here,
Here is himself, marred as you see with traitors.

FIRST CITIZEN: O piteous spectacle!

SECOND CITIZEN: O noble Cæsar!

THIRD CITIZEN: O woeful day!

FOURTH CITIZEN: O traitors, villains!

FIRST CITIZEN: O most bloody sight!

SECOND CITIZEN: We will be revenged.   200

ALL: Revenge! About! Seek! Burn! Fire! Kill! Slay!
Let not a traitor live!

ANTONY: Stay countrymen.

FIRST CITIZEN: Peace there, hear the noble Antony.

SECOND CITIZEN: We'll hear him, we'll follow him, we'll die
with him.

ANTONY: Good friends, sweet friends, let me not stir you up
To such a sudden flood of mutiny.
They that have done this deed are honourable.
What private griefs they have, alas, I know not,   210

212   *reasons*. An ironic echo of Brutus' words, ll. 7, 9, III. i. 236–7.

213– *I . . . is*. Antony contrasts himself with the conspirators implying
14   that they and Brutus in particular are skilled in the art of rousing
emotions whereas he has none of the arts of oratory. What is the
point of this disclaiming of oratorical skill—is it true, hypocritical,
to safeguard his actions, to imply that the citizens themselves have
seen and judged?

216–17 *and . . . him*. A hint at underhand business.

218–20 *wit . . . blood*, i.e. the qualities of an orator.

218   *wit*, intelligence. *words*, eloquence. *worth*, standing, reputation.

219   *Action*, gesture. *utterance*, delivery.

220   *right on*, straightforwardly.

225   *ruffle*, stir, i.e. as a dog raises his back hairs in anger or a cockerel
his neck feathers.

227   *stones . . . mutiny*. Perhaps an echo of *St. Luke*, xix. 40.

233–4 Antony makes sure that the citizens' fury is supported by the
knowledge of Cæsar's legacies to them.

240   *several*, individual.

241, 42 *noble Cæsar, royal Cæsar*. Compare ll. 47–8, 66.

That made them do it. They are wise and honourable,
And will no doubt with reasons answer you.
I come not friends, to steal away your hearts;
I am no orator as Brutus is;
But as you know me all, a plain blunt man,
That love my friend; and that they know full well
That gave me public leave to speak of him.
For I have neither wit, nor words, nor worth,
Action, nor utterance, nor the power of speech,
To stir men's blood; I only speak right on.   220
I tell you that which you yourselves do know,
Show you sweet Cæsar's wounds, poor poor dumb mouths,
And I bid them speak for me. But were I Brutus,
And Brutus Antony, there were an Antony
Would ruffle up your spirits, and put a tongue
In every wound of Cæsar that should move
The stones of Rome to rise and mutiny.

ALL: We'll mutiny.
FIRST CITIZEN: We'll burn the house of Brutus.
THIRD CITIZEN: Away then, come, seek the conspirators.   230
ANTONY: Yet hear me countrymen, yet hear me speak.
ALL: Peace ho, hear Antony, most noble Antony.
ANTONY: Why friends, you go to do you know not what.
    Wherein hath Cæsar thus deserved your loves?
    Alas you know not. I must tell you then.
    You have forgot the will I told you of.
ALL: Most true. The will, let's stay and hear the will.
ANTONY: Here is the will, and under Cæsar's seal.
    To every Roman citizen he gives,
    To every several man, seventy-five drachmas.   240
SECOND CITIZEN: Most noble Cæsar! We'll revenge his death.
THIRD CITIZEN: O royal Cæsar!
ANTONY: Hear me with patience.
ALL: Peace ho!

248   *common pleasures*, public pleasure-gardens.

257   *windows*, shutters (K. Tillotson.)
      The departure of the citizens should combine a dignified
      removal of Cæsar's body together with agitation and frenzy.

260   *Octavius . . . Rome*. Shakespeare again foreshortens the time of
      events. What is the dramatic gain?

264   *upon a wish*, just when I want him. *Fortune is merry*, the goddess
      Fortune is favourable.

268   *Belike . . . them*. A grim chuckle to accompany the understate-
      ment.
      What did Antony set out to do—restore Cæsar's reputation,
      avenge his death, obtain power for himself, cause a further
      bloodbath?
      Which words suit Antony—a self-seeker, unprincipled, re-
      sourceful, ambitious, unscrupulous, vicious, honourable, a genius,
      loyal, sincere, courageous, subtle, great?

ANTONY: Moreover, he hath left you all his walks,
  His private arbours and new-planted orchards,
  On this side Tiber; he hath left them you,
  And to your heirs for ever—common pleasures,
  To walk abroad, and recreate yourselves.
  Here was a Cæsar! When comes such another?   250
FIRST CITIZEN: Never, never. Come, away, away!
  We'll burn his body in the holy place,
  And with the brands fire the traitors' houses.
  Take up the body.
SECOND CITIZEN: Go fetch fire.
THIRD CITIZEN: Pluck down benches.
FOURTH CITIZEN: Pluck down forms, windows, any thing.
                              [*Exeunt Citizens with the body*
ANTONY: Now let it work. Mischief, thou art afoot,
  Take thou what course thou wilt.

Enter a SERVANT

                    How now, fellow!
SERVANT: Sir, Octavius is already come to Rome.   260
ANTONY: Where is he?
SERVANT: He and Lepidus are at Cæsar's house.
ANTONY: And thither will I straight to visit him.
  He comes upon a wish. Fortune is merry,
  And in this mood will give us anything.
SERVANT: I heard him say, Brutus and Cassius
  Are rid like madmen through the gates of Rome.
ANTONY: Belike they had some notice of the people,
  How I had moved them. Bring me to Octavius.   [*Exeunt*

Julius Cæsar

Rome. A street

Is Cinna edgy, nervous, furtive, fey, or somnambulistic? How does he walk?

Cinna, a poet of the period.

1 *tonight,* last night.

2 *unluckily . . . fantasy,* fill my imagination with foreboding. It was regarded as unlucky to dream of good fortune. (See *Merchant of Venice*, II. v, 16–18.)

5–12 This fusillade of questions shows the hungry ferocity of the citizens.

13–14 *What . . . bachelor.* How is this spoken—with drawling superiority, with fear and playing for time, with cool command of the situation, or playfully?

18 *You'll . . . that,* you'll gat a crack from me for that.

19 *directly,* keeping to the point.

27–9 *Tear . . . verses.* The mob is seeking a victim. Its brutal jeering, and lust for killing destroy Cinna because of his name. Is this murder parallel with the murder of Cæsar?

Presumably Cinna is killed off stage. How are the audience made aware of this?

What is the value of this scene—to give relief of action after speeches, underline the frightening fury of the mob, show the disorder and pitiless cruelty following Cæsar's death?

SCENE THREE

Enter CINNA *the poet, and after him* Citizens

CINNA: I dreamt tonight that I did feast with Cæsar,
And things unluckily charge my fantasy.
I have no will to wander forth of doors,
Yet something leads me forth.

FIRST CITIZEN: What is your name?

SECOND CITIZEN: Whither are you going?

THIRD CITIZEN: Where do you dwell?

FOURTH CITIZEN: Are you a married man or a bachelor?

SECOND CITIZEN: Answer every man directly.

FIRST CITIZEN: Ay, and briefly.   10

FOURTH CITIZEN: Ay, and wisely.

THIRD CITIZEN: Ay, and truly, you were best.

CINNA: What is my name? Whither am I going? Where do I dwell? Am I a married man or a bachelor? Then to answer every man directly and briefly, wisely and truly—wisely I say, I am a bachelor.

SECOND CITIZEN: That's as much as to say, they are fools that marry. You'll bear me a bang for that I fear. Proceed directly.

CINNA: Directly I am going to Cæsar's funeral.

FIRST CITIZEN: As a friend or an enemy?   20

CINNA: As a friend.

SECOND CITIZEN: That matter is answered directly.

FOURTH CITIZEN: For your dwelling—briefly.

CINNA: Briefly, I dwell by the Capitol.

THIRD CITIZEN: Your name sir, truly.

CINNA: Truly, my name is Cinna.

FIRST CITIZEN: Tear him to pieces, he's a conspirator.

CINNA: I am Cinna the poet, I am Cinna the poet.

FOURTH CITIZEN: Tear him for his bad verses, tear him for his bad verses.   30

CINNA: I am not Cinna the conspirator.

FOURTH CITIZEN: It is no matter, his name's Cinna; pluck but his name out of his heart, and turn him going.

THIRD CITIZEN: Tear him, tear him! Come, brands, ho! Fire brands. To Brutus', to Cassius'; burn all. Some to Decius' house, and some to Casca's; some to Ligarius'. Away, go!

[*Exeunt*

Rome. A room in Antony's house

Any stage property required? Do the three sit, recline or stand?

To the murder of one in hot blood in the last scene this scene adds murder of many in cold blood with the excuse of revenge for Cæsar's murder, or is it to secure power?

1   *These . . . pricked.* A grim, callous sentence that strikes the note for the whole scene. *pricked,* marked by a hole pricked through the paper.

2   *Your brother,* Lucius Aemilius Paulus, who, however, escaped and joined Brutus, but was afterwards pardoned.

4–5   *Upon . . . Antony.* Is this bargaining meant to show—Lepidus' small-mindedness, Antony's impartiality or his indifference, or the contrast between Antony and Octavius?

4   *Publius.* Shakespeare's addition.

6   *with . . . him.* How is this done—with a stylus, quill, sword or dagger; with a flourish, in silence, or with a heavy sound? *spot,* (*a*) prick, (*b*) mark, with perhaps a glance at 'spot'=sin. *damn,* condemn, doom.

7   *go . . . house.* Perhaps a slip. See III. ii, 262–3.

9   *cut . . . legacies,* cut down payment of some of the sums of money bequeathed by Cæsar. Antony in a dangerous situation (ll. 48–51) is unscrupulous about appropriating this money.

10   *What . . . here?* How should Lepidus be characterized—inane, foppish, effeminate, 'blimpish', or suspicious and rat-like?

12–13   *This . . . errands.* Any gesture?

12   *slight,* worthless. *unmeritable,* not worth considering.

14   *The . . . divided,* the Roman empire being shared into three portions, i.e. Europe, Africa and Asia.

These three men, the triumvirs, shared the government of the empire.

ACT FOUR

SCENE ONE

ANTONY, OCTAVIUS, *and* LEPIDUS, *seated at a table*

ANTONY: These many then shall die; their names are pricked.
OCTAVIUS: Your brother too must die; consent you Lepidus?
LEPIDUS: I do consent—
OCTAVIUS: Prick him down Antony.
LEPIDUS: Upon condition Publius shall not live,
   Who is your sister's son, Mark Antony.
ANTONY: He shall not live; look, with a spot I damn him.
   But Lepidus, go you to Cæsar's house;
   Fetch the will hither, and we shall determine
   How to cut off some charge in legacies.
LEPIDUS: What, shall I find you here?   10
OCTAVIUS: Or here, or at the Capitol.   [*Exit Lepidus*
ANTONY: This is a slight unmeritable man,
   Meet to be sent on errands. Is it fit,
   The three-fold world divided, he should stand
   One of the three to share it?

15–17 *So ... proscription.* Is this—contemptuous, indignant, accusing, sneering, ironic, naive or priggish?

16 *took his voice,* accepted his opinion.

17 *black sentence,* i.e. sentence of death. *proscription,* list of those condemned to death.

20 *To ... loads,* to take from our shoulders the weight of various slanderous accusations. i.e. Lepidus would take the blame for some of their actions that would rouse enmity.

21 *them,* (a) honours, (b) slanders. *as ... gold.* Proverbial. The point is that the ass carries gold in ignorance of its nature and but for a short time.

26 *shake his ears,* be off with him. Proverbial.

27 *in commons,* on free grazing land.

30 *appoint,* provide.

32 *wind,* turn, wheel.

33 *His ... spirit,* his bodily movements controlled by my mind, i.e. even as the soul directs the physical movements in men. Stress 'His' and 'my'.

34 *taste,* measure.

36 *barren-spirited,* dull, lacking imagination.

36–7 *feeds On,* stuffs his mind with.

37 *objects,* ideas or curiosities. *arts,* devices or artifices. Some editors prefer to read 'abject orts' (cast off scraps) for the Folio reading 'objects, arts'.

38 *staled,* made common, hackneyed.

39 *Begin his fashion,* are the starting point of his ideas, or, are taken by him as up-to-date.

40 *property,* tool.

42 *powers,* armies. *make head,* gather our forces.

44 *made,* ensured, secured. *our means stretched,* our resources strained to the uttermost.

45 *presently,* at once.

46 *covert ... disclosed,* secret dangers may best be brought to light.

47 *answered,* dealt with, met.

OCTAVIUS: So you thought him,
 And took his voice who should be pricked to die,
 In our black sentence and proscription.
ANTONY: Octavius, I have seen more days than you;
 And though we lay these honours on this man,
 To ease ourselves of divers sland'rous loads,   20
 He shall but bear them as the ass bears gold,
 To groan and sweat under the business,
 Either led or driven, as we point the way;
 And having brought our treasure where we will,
 Then take we down his load, and turn him off,
 Like to the empty ass, to shake his ears,
 And graze in commons.
OCTAVIUS: You may do your will;
 But he's a tried and valiant soldier.
ANTONY: So is my horse Octavius, and for that
 I do appoint him store of provender.   30
 It is a creature that I teach to fight,
 To wind, to stop, to run directly on,
 His corporal motion governed by my spirit.
 And, in some taste, is Lepidus but so;
 He must be taught, and trained, and bid go forth.
 A barren-spirited fellow; one that feeds
 On objects, arts, and imitations,
 Which, out of use and staled by other men,
 Begin his fashion. Do not talk of him
 But as a property. And now Octavius,   40
 Listen great things. Brutus and Cassius
 Are levying powers; we must straight make head.
 Therefore let our alliance be combined,
 Our best friends made, our means stretched;
 And let us presently go sit in council,
 How covert matters may be best disclosed,
 And open perils surest answered.

48–9   *at . . . enemies,* i.e. in a hazardous position beset with enemies, as a bear tied to the stake is set upon by dogs.

51   *mischiefs,* harmful thoughts.

Before Brutus' tent near Sardis

s.d.   The Arden reading has been adopted in place of the misleading Folio directions.

A brisk bustling opening with men marching and orders shouted. Brutus emerging from his tent meets Lucilius with his men.

1   *Stand ho!* halt! *ho,* halt, stop.

2   *Give . . . stand.* Lucilius repeats the order to his men.

5   *To . . . salutation,* to give you greetings.

6   *He . . . well,* i.e. greetings borne by so noble a messenger as Pindarus are welcome. Kittredge notes that Brutus is always courteous to subordinates.

7   *In . . . officers,* either because he has changed his views, or because he has been ill-served by his officers.

8   *worthy,* weighty, serious.

10   *be satisfied,* be given a satisfactory explanation.

12   *full . . . honour,* highly respected and honourable.

13   *A word, Lucilius.* Any action or gesture?

14   *resolved,* clear about it.

16   *familiar instances,* signs of friendliness.

17   *conference,* conversation.

OCTAVIUS: Let us do so; for we are at the stake,
    And bayed about with many enemies;
    And some that smile have in their hearts, I fear,   50
    Millions of mischiefs.   *[Exeunt*

SCENE TWO

Drum. Enter BRUTUS, LUCILIUS, LUCIUS, *and* Soldiers, TITINIUS
and PINDARUS *meet them*

BRUTUS: Stand ho!
LUCILIUS: Give the word ho! and stand.
BRUTUS: What now Lucilius, is Cassius near?
LUCILIUS: He is at hand, and Pindarus is come
    To do you salutation from his master.
BRUTUS: He greets me well. Your master, Pindarus,
    In his own change, or by ill officers,
    Hath given me some worthy cause to wish
    Things done, undone. But if he be at hand,
    I shall be satisfied.
PINDARUS: I do not doubt   10
    But that my noble master will appear
    Such as he is, full of regard and honour.
BRUTUS: He is not doubted. A word Lucilius;
    How he received you, let me be resolved.
LUCILIUS: With courtesy, and with respect enough,
    But not with such familiar instances,
    Nor with such free and friendly conference,
    As he hath used of old.

20   *love*, friendship.

21   *enforced ceremony*, forced politeness.

23   *hollow*, insincere. *hot at hand*, burning with eagerness at first.

26   *fall their crests*, lower their arched necks. *fall*, let fall. *crests*. A high arching neck was regarded as a sign of a spirited horse. *jades*, worthless horses.

27   *sink*, fail.

29   *horse*, cavalry.
       Another entry with military spectacle, sounds and movement. The suspicions voiced by Brutus rouse a feeling of suspense and tension.

S.D.   *Powers*, army, forces.

37   *Most . . . wrong*. Cassius is smarting under a feeling of injustice.

38–9   *Judge . . . brother*, if I do not wrong even my enemies, how can I possibly wrong my brother (Cassius)? Brutus confident in his own honest dealing is taken aback by the unexpectedness of Cassius' accusation.

40   *sober form*, dignified bearing.

41   *be content*, keep calm.

42   *griefs*, grievances. *do know*, understand.

46   *enlarge*, speak freely of.
       A second time in an emergency Brutus keeps his head better than Cassius. (See III. i, 22–4.)

BRUTUS: Thou hast described
  A hot friend cooling. Ever note Lucilius,
  When love begins to sicken and decay   20
  It useth an enforced ceremony.
  There are no tricks in plain and simple faith;
  But hollow men, like horses hot at hand,
  Make gallant show and promise of their mettle;
                            [*Low march within*
  But when they should endure the bloody spur,
  They fall their crests, and like deceitful jades
  Sink in the trial. Comes his army on?
LUCILIUS: They mean this night in Sardis to be quartered.
  The greater part, the horse in general,
  Are come with Cassius.
BRUTUS: Hark, he is arrived.   30
  March gently on to meet him.

Enter CASSIUS *and his Powers*

CASSIUS: Stand ho!
BRUTUS: Stand ho! Speak the word along.
FIRST SOLDIER: Stand!
SECOND SOLDIER: Stand!
THIRD SOLDIER: Stand!
CASSIUS: Most noble brother, you have done me wrong.
BRUTUS: Judge me you gods; wrong I mine enemies?
  And if not so, how should I wrong a brother?
CASSIUS: Brutus, this sober form of yours hides wrongs,   40
  And when you do them—
BRUTUS: Cassius, be content,
  Speak your griefs softly, I do know you well.
  Before the eyes of both our armies here,
  Which should perceive nothing but love from us,
  Let us not wrangle. Bid them move away.
  Then in my tent Cassius, enlarge your griefs,

48   *charges*, forces, troops.

50, 52 *Lucius, Lucilius*. Editors generally prefer these readings in place of the Folio readings, 'Lucilius', 'Let Lucius'.

Within Brutus' tent

The conventional division into a new scene here has been retained for ease of cross-reference to other editions or critical works. There is obviously no change of scene; Brutus and Cassius probably enter a 'mansion' or 'house' on the stage.

2   *noted*, branded with disgrace.

4   *Wherein*, in which affair.

5   *slighted off*, contemptuously pushed aside.

8   *That . . . comment*, that every trivial offence should be subjected to an inquiry. *his*; its.

10   *condemned . . . palm*, accused of being ready to accept bribes.

11   *mart*, drive bargains, traffic in.

15–16 *The . . . head*, the high reputation of Cassius glosses over such corrupt activities, and no punishment therefore is forthcoming.

And I will give you audience.

CASSIUS: Pindarus,
Bid our commanders lead their charges off
A little from this ground.

BRUTUS: Lucius, do you the like; and let no man   50
Come to our tent till we have done our conference.
Lucilius and Titinius guard our door.   [*Exeunt*

SCENE THREE

BRUTUS *and* CASSIUS *enter the tent*

CASSIUS: That you have wronged me doth appear in this:
You have condemned and noted Lucius Pella
For taking bribes here of the Sardians;
Wherein my letters, praying on his side,
Because I knew the man, were slighted off.

BRUTUS: You wronged yourself to write in such a case.

CASSIUS: In such a time as this it is not meet
That every nice offence should bear his comment.

BRUTUS: Let me tell you Cassius, you yourself
Are much condemned to have an itching palm,   10
To sell and mart your offices for gold
To undeservers.

CASSIUS: I an itching palm!
You know that you are Brutus that speak this,
Or by the gods, this speech were else your last.

BRUTUS: The name of Cassius honours this corruption,
And chastisement doth therefore hide his head.

18   *Remember . . . remember.* Emphatic. See III. ii, 13–17 for a similar construction.

19   *for justice' sake.* Has Brutus changed his opinions since the murder? Justice was not then mentioned. Is there a dramatic reason for introducing it here?

20–1   *What . . . justice,* was anyone so villainous as to stab him not as an act of justice, but from baser motives?

23   *But . . . robbers,* because he supported robbers. An additional reason for killing Cæsar which Shakespeare took from Plutarch's account of the quarrel.

25   *the . . . honours,* the wide range of our offices of honour in the state.

26   *trash,* rubbish, worthless money. *grasped thus.* Perhaps a gesture to emphasize the image of 'itching palm' and contaminated 'fingers'.

27   *bay,* howl at.

28   *bait not me,* do not hound me, i.e. as a dog attacks a chained bear.

30   *To . . . in,* to restrict my freedom of action. *I . . . I.* Emphatic.

31   *practice,* experience.

32   *To make conditions,* to decide matters, to deal with such affairs.

       The quarrel degenerates. Cassius' claim to superiority in military experience and perhaps his gestures and intonation rouse Brutus to denial and personal insult.

35   *Urge,* provoke.

36   *health,* welfare. *tempt me,* try my patience.

37   *slight man,* worthless creature.

39   *give . . . choler,* allow your bad temper free utterance and scope.

40   *stares,* glowers, glares. i.e. Cassius' threats ll. 14, 35–6 have provoked this from Brutus.

42   *Fret.* By what gestures and movement does Cassius reveal his fretting?

45   *observe,* humble myself for. *stand,* put up with.

46   *testy humour,* quarrelsome mood.

47   *digest . . . spleen,* swallow your own poisonous bad temper. The spleen was regarded as the seat of ill-humour and of mirth.

CASSIUS: Chastisement?

BRUTUS: Remember March, the ides of March remember.
Did not great Julius bleed for justice' sake?
What villain touched his body, that did stab,   20
And not for justice? What, shall one of us,
That struck the foremost man of all this world
But for supporting robbers, shall we now
Contaminate our fingers with base bribes,
And sell the mighty space of our large honours
For so much trash as may be grasped thus?
I had rather be a dog, and bay the moon,
Than such a Roman.

CASSIUS: Brutus, bait not me,
I'll not endure it. You forget yourself,
To hedge me in. I am a soldier, I,   30
Older in practice, abler than yourself
To make conditions.

BRUTUS: Go to! You are not, Cassius.

CASSIUS: I am.

BRUTUS: I say you are not.

CASSIUS: Urge me no more, I shall forget myself;
Have mind upon your health; tempt me no farther.

BRUTUS: Away slight man.

CASSIUS: Is't possible?

BRUTUS: Hear me, for I will speak.
Must I give way and room to your rash choler?
Shall I be frighted when a madman stares?   40

CASSIUS: O ye gods, ye gods! must I endure all this?

BRUTUS: All this? Ay, more. Fret till your proud heart break.
Go show your slaves how choleric you are,
And make bondmen tremble. Must I budge?
Must I observe you? must I stand and crouch
Under your testy humour? By the gods,
You shall digest the venom of your spleen,

48   *split,* (a) with great pain or (b) with excessive laughter.
49   *mirth,* laughing-stock.

52   *vaunting,* boasting.

54   *noble men.* Does this imply that Cassius is not noble?

57   *If . . . not.* Is Brutus unfair, indifferent, pugnacious, ill-humoured, splenetic, justified?
58   *moved,* roused.
59   *tempted,* provoked.

62   *For . . . not.* Is Cassius a coward, or is Brutus mistaken or deliberately contemptuous?

67   *For . . . honesty,* for my high principles so protect me, for I am so confident my views are honourable.
68   *idle,* empty.

71   *vile,* unworthy.

73   *drachmas.* Ancient Greek silver coins.
74   *vile trash,* wretched cash.
75   *indirection,* crooked dealing.

Though it do split you. For from this day forth,
I'll use you for my mirth, yea for my laughter,
When you are waspish.

CASSIUS: Is it come to this? 50

BRUTUS: You say you are a better soldier.
Let it appear so; make your vaunting true,
And it shall please me well. For mine own part,
I shall be glad to learn of noble men.

CASSIUS: You wrong me every way; you wrong me Brutus.
I said, an elder soldier, not a better.
Did I say better?

BRUTUS: If you did, I care not.

CASSIUS: When Cæsar lived, he durst not thus have moved me.

BRUTUS: Peace, peace, you durst not so have tempted him.

CASSIUS: I durst not? 60

BRUTUS: No.

CASSIUS: What, durst not tempt him?

BRUTUS: For your life you durst not.

CASSIUS: Do not presume too much upon my love;
I may do that I shall be sorry for.

BRUTUS: You have done that you should be sorry for.
There is no terror, Cassius, in your threats;
For I am armed so strong in honesty
That they pass by me as the idle wind,
Which I respect not. I did send to you
For certain sums of gold, which you denied me; 70
For I can raise no money by vile means.
By heaven, I had rather coin my heart,
And drop my blood for drachmas, than to wring
From the hard hands of peasants their vile trash
By any indirection. I did send
To you for gold to pay my legions,
Which you denied me. Was that done like Cassius?
Should I have answered Caius Cassius so?

80   *rascal counters*, worthless pieces.

85   *rived*, broken.

88   *practise*, impose.

92   *Olympus*. See III. i, 74.

93–   *Come ... Cassius*. What feelings is Cassius' reference to himself in
107   the third person intended to make plain? Compare Cæsar's
      references to himself II. ii, 28–9, etc.

96   *braved*, defied.

97   *Checked*, rebuked.

98   *conned by rote*, learnt by heart.

99–   *O ... Cassius*. Any response in gesture or movement from Brutus
107   to Cassius' offer in readiness for the conciliatory tone of his next
      speech?

102   *Pluto's mine*. Pluto, the classical god of Hades, and Plutus the god
      of wealth were frequently confused.

108   *it ... scope*, it shall go unchecked.

When Marcus Brutus grows so covetous,
To lock such rascal counters from his friends,   80
Be ready gods with all your thunderbolts:
Dash him to pieces.

CASSIUS: I denied you not.

BRUTUS: You did.

CASSIUS: I did not. He was but a fool that brought
My answer back. Brutus hath rived my heart.
A friend should bear his friend's infirmities;
But Brutus makes mine greater than they are.

BRUTUS: I do not, till you practise them on me.

CASSIUS: You love me not.

BRUTUS: I do not like your faults.

CASSIUS: A friendly eye could never see such faults.   90

BRUTUS: A flatterer's would not, though they do appear
As huge as high Olympus.

CASSIUS: Come Antony, and young Octavius come,
Revenge yourselves alone on Cassius,
For Cassius is aweary of the world:
Hated by one he loves; braved by his brother;
Checked like a bondman; all his faults observed,
Set in a note-book, learned, and conned by rote,
To cast into my teeth. O I could weep
My spirit from mine eyes. There is my dagger,   100
And here my naked breast; within, a heart
Dearer than Pluto's mine, richer than gold.
If that thou be'st a Roman, take it forth.
I that denied thee gold, will give my heart.
Strike as thou didst at Cæsar. For I know,
When thou didst hate him worst, thou lovedst him better
Than ever thou lovedst Cassius.

BRUTUS: Sheathe your dagger.
Be angry when you will, it shall have scope.

109   *dishonour . . . humour*, any shame you lay on me will be taken as the expression of a passing mood.

112   *much enforced*, violently struck.

115   *blood ill-tempered*, unbalanced feeling. i.e. his blood contained too much 'choler'.

118   *O Brutus!* Is Cassius overwhelmed by relief, agitation, grief or love? Any action?

120   *rash humour*, quick temper.

122   *over-earnest*. A tactful understatement.
     How should the Poet enter—quietly, struggling with the guards, noisily, wildly, timidly, vociferously?

131-2 *Love . . . ye*. This couplet is a version of a couplet in North's Plutarch, and a translation of words spoken by Nestor in Homer's *Iliad*. Is the couplet meant seriously, or in jest?

133   *cynic*, philosopher. The Cynics were philosophers who condemned ease and luxury and were given to fault-finding.

134   *Get . . . hence*. Brutus is irritable again: Cassius laughs. Has Brutus a sense of humour?

Do what you will, dishonour shall be humour.   110
O Cassius, you are yoked with a lamb
That carries anger as the flint bears fire,
Who much enforced shows a hasty spark,
And straight is cold again.

CASSIUS: Hath Cassius lived
To be but mirth and laughter to his Brutus,
When grief and blood ill-tempered vexeth him?

BRUTUS: When I spoke that, I was ill-tempered too.

CASSIUS: Do you confess so much? Give me your hand.

BRUTUS: And my heart too.

CASSIUS: O Brutus

BRUTUS: What's the matter?

CASSIUS: Have not you love enough to bear with me,
When that rash humour which my mother gave me   120
Makes me forgetful?

BRUTUS: Yes Cassius, and from henceforth,
When you are over-earnest with your Brutus,
He'll think your mother chides, and leave you so.

Enter POET, *followed by* LUCILIUS, TITINIUS, *and*
LUCIUS

POET: Let me go in to see the generals.
There is some grudge between 'em, 'tis not meet
They be alone.

LUCILIUS: You shall not come to them.

POET: Nothing but death shall stay me.

CASSIUS: How now? What's the matter?

POET: For shame you generals, what do you mean?   130
Love, and be friends, as two such men should be,
For I have seen more years I'm sure than ye.

CASSIUS: Ha, ha, how vilely doth this cynic rhyme!

BRUTUS: Get you hence sirrah. Saucy fellow, hence!

CASSIUS: Bear with him Brutus, 'tis his fashion.

136   *I'll . . . time*, I will accept his foolery when he chooses the right time to present it.

137   *What . . . fools*, i.e. war is a serious business in which there is no place for these silly rhymers.

138   *Companion*, wretched fellow.

       Is the Poet's departure dignified, comic, assisted by the guards, bewildered? What purpose does the intrusion of the Poet serve— break the tension, to confirm the reconciliation between Brutus and Cassius, to jar and irritate Brutus almost beyond endurance with trivialities, to show how Brutus conceals private feelings from his followers, to create a change of mood so that the news of Portia's death comes with the greater shock?

140   *lodge*, encamp.

144   *O . . . griefs*. Brutus breaks down; Cassius has recovered his poise.

145–6   *Of . . . evils*, i.e. Brutus, as a follower of the Stoic philosophy should not give way to chance sorrows.

147   *No . . . better*. Is Brutus boastful, conceited, goaded beyond endurance, anguished? *Portia is dead*. Is this spoken with slow deliberation, hesitatingly, harshly, rapidly, or firmly?

150   *crossed*, defied.

151   *touching*, sorrowful. Any movement or gesture?

152–3   *Impatient . . . grief*, unable to endure my absence and out of sorrow.

154–5   *for . . . came*, for with the news of her death came that information as well.

155   *distract*, out of her mind, beside herself.

156   *swallowed fire*. According to Plutarch 'hot burning coals'.

       Do Brutus and Cassius drink from the same bowl or from separate bowls?

BRUTUS: I'll know his humour, when he knows his time.
What should the wars do with these jigging fools?
Companion, hence!
CASSIUS: Away, away, be gone.   [*Exit Poet*
BRUTUS: Lucilius and Titinius, bid the commanders
Prepare to lodge their companies tonight.   140
CASSIUS: And come yourselves, and bring Messala with you
Immediately to us.   [*Exeunt Lucilius and Titinius*
BRUTUS: Lucius, a bowl of wine.   [*Exit Lucius*
CASSIUS: I did not think you could have been so angry.
BRUTUS: O Cassius, I am sick of many griefs.
CASSIUS: Of your philosophy you make no use,
If you give place to accidental evils.
BRUTUS: No man bears sorrow better. Portia is dead.
CASSIUS: Ha! Portia?
BRUTUS: She is dead.
CASSIUS: How 'scaped I killing when I crossed you so?   150
O insupportable and touching loss!
Upon what sickness?
BRUTUS: Impatient of my absence,
And grief that young Octavius with Mark Antony
Have made themselves so strong; for with her death
That tidings came. With this she fell distract,
And, her attendants absent, swallowed fire.
CASSIUS: And died so?
BRUTUS: Even so.
CASSIUS: O ye immortal gods!

Enter LUCIUS *with wine and tapers*

BRUTUS: Speak no more of her. Give me a bowl of wine.
In this I bury all unkindness Cassius.
CASSIUS: My heart is thirsty for that noble pledge.   160
Fill Lucius, till the wine o'erswell the cup.
I cannot drink too much of Brutus' love.

165   *call ... necessities,* inquire into our army's needs.

169   *power,* army.

170   *Philippi,* a town in Macedonia.

171   *tenor,* effect, trend.

173   *proscription,* sentence of death.

181– Most editors retain these lines but consider that in the manu-
95 script copy they were marked for omission, and that ll. 142–57,
165 were substituted. The compositor, however, failed to notice
the deletion marks and printed both versions. They stress the incon-
sistency between Brutus' account of Portia's death in ll. 142–57
and his denial of any knowledge of it here. Other writers hold that
this second account is a most skilful piece of dramatic writing that
enriches the whole scene.

Are the two accounts complementary? If either were omitted,
what view of Brutus would remain? Is the second account em-
blematic, to save appearances, expedient, hypocritical, melo-
dramatic posturing, to support the stoic myth of Brutus, to
establish confidence in Brutus' resolution?

BRUTUS: Come in Titinius.   [*Exit Lucius*

        Enter LUCILIUS, TITINIUS, *with* MESSALA
                  Welcome good Messala.
  Now sit we close about this taper here,
  And call in question our necessities.
CASSIUS: Portia, art thou gone?
BRUTUS: No more I pray you.
  Messala, I have here received letters,
  That young Octavius and Mark Antony
  Come down upon us with a mighty power,
  Bending their expedition toward Philippi.   170
MESSALA: Myself have letters of the selfsame tenor.
BRUTUS: With what addition?
MESSALA: That by proscription and bills of outlawry,
  Octavius, Antony, and Lepidus,
  Have put to death an hundred senators.
BRUTUS: Therein our letters do not well agree.
  Mine speak of seventy senators that died
  By their proscriptions, Cicero being one.
CASSIUS: Cicero one?
MESSALA: Cicero is dead,
  And by that order of proscription.   180
  Had you your letters from your wife, my lord?
BRUTUS: No Messala.
MESSALA: Nor nothing in your letters writ of her?
BRUTUS: Nothing Messala.
MESSALA: That methinks is strange.
BRUTUS: Why ask you? Hear you aught of her in yours?
MESSALA: No my lord.
BRUTUS: Now as you are a Roman tell me true.
MESSALA: Then like a Roman bear the truth I tell,
  For certain she is dead, and by strange manner.
BRUTUS: Why farewell Portia. We must die, Messala.   190

191 *With . . . once.* See Cæsar's comment II. ii, 36–7. *once,* at one time
or another.

194 *I . . . you,* I am as well acquainted with the theory of repressing
my feelings as you are.

196 *alive,* i.e. after all the talk of death Brutus speaks briskly and cheer-
fully.

197 *presently,* at once.

201 *offence,* harm.

202 *defence,* i.e. well-defended. *nimbleness,* i.e. active and fresh.

203 *of force,* of necessity. Is Brutus insensitive, frank, obstinate, complacent, or self-satisfied?

205 *stand . . . affection,* give us their good will only because they are
forced to do so.

206 *contribution,* i.e. of men and provisions.

209 *new-added,* with reinforcements.

213 *Under your pardon.* Brutus cuts Cassius short. (See III. i, 235 ff;
II. i, 162 ff.)

217 *height,* i.e. of our fortunes.

218 *tide,* (*a*) flood tide, (*b*) time.

220 *Omitted,* missed, neglected.

221 *bound in,* (*a*) set course in, (*b*) confined to. *shallows,* (*a*) low water,
(*b*) petty hindrances. *miseries,* wretchedness, i.e. the opposite of
fortune.

With meditating that she must die once,
I have the patience to endure it now.
MESSALA: Even so great men great losses should endure.
CASSIUS: I have as much of this in art as you,
But yet my nature could not bear it so.
BRUTUS: Well, to our work alive. What do you think
Of marching to Philippi presently?
CASSIUS: I do not think it good.
BRUTUS: Your reason?
CASSIUS: This it is:
'Tis better that the enemy seek us;
So shall he waste his means, weary his soldiers,   200
Doing himself offence, whilst we lying still,
Are full of rest, defence, and nimbleness.
BRUTUS: Good reasons must of force give place to better.
The people 'twixt Philippi and this ground
Do stand but in a forced affection;
For they have grudged us contribution.
The enemy, marching along by them,
By them shall make a fuller number up,
Come on refreshed, new-added, and encouraged;
From which advantage shall we cut him off,   210
If at Philippi we do face him there,
These people at our back.
CASSIUS: Hear me good brother.
BRUTUS: Under your pardon. You must note beside,
That we have tried the utmost of our friends,
Our legions are brim-full, our cause is ripe.
The enemy increaseth every day;
We, at the height, are ready to decline.
There is a tide in the affairs of men,
Which taken at the flood leads on to fortune;
Omitted, all the voyage of their life   220
Is bound in shallows and in miseries.

224 *ventures*, merchant vessels or merchandise out at risk.
The complex imagery in this speech is presumably effective in convincing the others. See II. i, 114–40, 162–83. See also Introduction p. 24.

224 *with your will*, as you wish to have it.

226 *The . . . talk*. Is this symbolical, or to prepare for what follows?

227 *necessity*, need for sleep.

228 *niggard*, restrict, limit.

231 *gown*, robe, dressing-gown.

232 *Noble, noble*. What feelings does the repetition imply?

233–6 *O . . . well*. Presumably spoken aside.

235 *division . . . souls*. True friends had 'one soul in bodies twain'.

237 *my lord*. This touch of reverence Brutus delicately repays with 'good brother' (Wilson and Barker).

239 *instrument*, lute.

240 *Here . . . tent*. Brutus had seen his friends out of the tent when they departed. How do Lucius' words call forth Brutus' comment?

241 *knave*, boy. *o'er-watched*, tired out by keeping awake.

On such a full sea are we now afloat,
And we must take the current when it serves,
Or lose our ventures.
CASSIUS: Then with your will go on.
We'll along ourselves, and meet them at Philippi.
BRUTUS: The deep of night is crept upon our talk,
And nature must obey necessity,
Which we will niggard with a little rest.
There is no more to say.
CASSIUS: No more. Good night:
Early tomorrow will we rise, and hence.   230
BRUTUS: Lucius! [*Enter Lucius*] My gown. [*Exit Lucius*] Fare-
well good Messala:
Good night Titinius. Noble, noble Cassius,
Good night, and good repose.
CASSIUS: O my dear brother!
This was an ill beginning of the night.
Never come such division 'tween our souls!
Let it not Brutus.

Enter LUCIUS *with gown*

BRUTUS: Every thing is well.
CASSIUS: Good night my lord.
BRUTUS: Good night good brother.
TITINIUS, MESSALA: Good night Lord Brutus.
BRUTUS: Farewell every one.
                    [*Exeunt Cassius, Titinius, Lucilius and Messala*
Give me the gown. Where is thy instrument?
LUCIUS: Here in the tent.
BRUTUS: What, thou speak'st drowsily?   240
Poor knave, I blame thee not; thou art o'erwatched.
Call Claudius and some other of my men;
I'll have them sleep on cushions in my tent.
LUCIUS: Varro and Claudius!

246–8 *I . . . Cassius.* What dramatic point has the presence of these men —to illustrate Brutus' care for his servants, to establish the nature of Brutus' visitor, to show Brutus' forethought?

247 *raise*, rouse.

249 *watch your pleasure*, (a) attend to your wishes, (b) remain awake at your disposal.

251 *otherwise bethink me*, change my mind.

252–5 *Look . . . forgetful.* What effect is aimed at—to show Brutus' scholarly interests, his humanity and kindliness, to provide touches of realism, to recall an atmosphere of harmony, to lead up to the arrival of Cæsar's ghost?

266 Brutus reclines or sits to listen to the song.

267 *murd'rous slumber*, sleep that cuts short the harmony. There may be also a glance at the often mentioned resemblance between a sleeping person and a dead person.

268 *leaden mace*, (a) the sheriff's officer had a mace with which he touched the person to be arrested, (b) there is also a glance at the wand of Morpheus, the god of sleep.

271–2 *If . . . thee.* Is this a touch of affection for Lucius or does it symbolize a last attempt to preserve the right harmony of things?

Enter VARRO *and* CLAUDIUS

VARRO: Calls my lord?

BRUTUS: I pray you sirs, lie in my tent and sleep;
　It may be I shall raise you by and by
　On business to my brother Cassius.

VARRO: So please you, we will stand and watch your pleasure.

BRUTUS: I will not have it so. Lie down good sirs;　　　　250
　It may be I shall otherwise bethink me.
　Look Lucius, here's the book I sought for so;
　I put it in the pocket of my gown.

LUCIUS: I was sure your lordship did not give it me.

BRUTUS: Bear with me good boy, I am much forgetful.
　Canst thou hold up thy heavy eyes awhile,
　And touch thy instrument a strain or two?

LUCIUS: Ay my lord, an't please you.

BRUTUS:　　　　　　　　　　　　It does, my boy.
　I trouble thee too much, but thou art willing.

LUCIUS: It is my duty sir.　　　　　　　　　　260

BRUTUS: I should not urge thy duty past thy might;
　I know young bloods look for a time of rest.

LUCIUS: I have slept my lord already.

BRUTUS: It was well done, and thou shalt sleep again;
　I will not hold thee long. If I do live,
　I will be good to thee.　　　　　[*Music and a song*
　This is a sleepy tune. O murd'rous slumber,
　Layest thou thy leaden mace upon my boy,
　That plays thee music? Gentle knave good night;
　I will not do thee so much wrong to wake thee.　　　　270
　If thou dost nod, thou break'st thy instrument;
　I'll take it from thee; and, good boy, good night.
　Let me see, let me see; is not the leaf turned down
　Where I left reading? Here it is, I think.

275   *ill . . . burns*. It was believed that lights burned dim or blue in the presence of a ghost.

277   *monstrous*, unnatural, fearful.
        Does Brutus rise, move or respond in any way?

278   *thing*, being of any kind.

279   *angel*, spirit.

280   *stare*, stand on end with fear.

282   *evil spirit*, i.e. that has driven away Brutus' good spirit or Cæsar's powerful spirit that is dominating Brutus' spirit.

285   *shall*, must.

287   *will*, am content to.

287-8   *Why . . . vanishest*. Any change in pitch, speed or intonation to support this?

292   *The . . . false*. What is the point of this—Lucius' unconscious fear, a comment on the prevailing disorder and disharmony, a symbolic parallel to the appearance of the ghost. *false*, out of tune.

304   *Why . . . sleep?* What is Brutus testing?

Enter the Ghost of CÆSAR

How ill this taper burns. Ha! Who comes here?
I think it is the weakness of mine eyes
That shapes this monstrous apparition.
It comes upon me. Art thou any thing?
Art thou some god, some angel, or some devil,
That mak'st my blood cold, and my hair to stare?   280
Speak to me what thou art.

GHOST: Thy evil spirit Brutus.

BRUTUS: Why com'st thou?

GHOST: To tell thee thou shalt see me at Philippi.

BRUTUS: Well; then I shall see thee again?

GHOST: Ay, at Philippi.

BRUTUS: Why I will see thee at Philippi then.   [*Exit Ghost*
Now I have taken heart thou vanishest.
Ill spirit, I would hold more talk with thee.
Boy, Lucius! Varro! Claudius! Sirs, awake.   290
Claudius!

LUCIUS: The strings, my lord, are false.

BRUTUS: He thinks he still is at his instrument.
Lucius, awake.

LUCIUS: My lord.

BRUTUS: Didst thou dream, Lucius, that thou so criedst out?

LUCIUS: My lord, I do not know that I did cry.

BRUTUS: Yes that thou didst. Didst thou see any thing?

LUCIUS: Nothing my lord.

BRUTUS: Sleep again Lucius. Sirrah Claudius!   [*To* VARRO]
Fellow thou, awake!   301

VARRO: My lord.

CLAUDIUS: My lord.

BRUTUS: Why did you so cry out sirs, in your sleep?

VARRO, CLAUDIUS: Did we my lord?

BRUTUS: Ay. Saw you any thing?

308   *betimes*, early.

In this episode of the ghost what qualities does Brutus show—courage, fear, self-control, panic, resignation, despair, curiosity?

VARRO: No my lord, I saw nothing.

CLAUDIUS: Nor I my lord.

BRUTUS: Go and commend me to my brother Cassius.
  Bid him set on his powers betimes before,   308
  And we will follow.

BOTH: It shall be done my lord.   [*Exeunt*

The Plains of Philippi

A full martial entry with trumpets, drums and banners.

1–12   *Now . . . so.* Is Octavius mildly triumphant, self-satisfied, complacent, mocking, arrogant, maliciously enjoying himself?

4   *battles,* armies.

5   *warn,* defy, challenge.

6   *Answering . . . them,* accepting battle before we have defied them.

7   *Tut.* Is this an expression of impatience, irritation, embarrassment or contempt? *I . . . bosoms,* I can read their thoughts.

8–9   *could . . . places,* would gladly be elsewhere (Arden).

10   *fearful bravery,* (a) a brave show to hide their fear, or (b) a brave show to frighten us. *face,* show.

10–11   *face To fasten.* Is this a quibble?

14   *bloody . . . out.* According to Plutarch the signal was an 'arming scarlet coat'. Shakespeare elsewhere uses 'bloody flag' as a sign of battle.

16–20   *Octavius . . . so.* What does this show—Octavius' obstinacy, strong will, good judgement, pettiness, assumption of authority? Is it symbolic of their fortunes afterwards that Octavius takes the righthand or fortunate side, or is the episode a hint of future disagreement?

16   *softly,* slowly.

19   *cross,* thwart, disagree with. *exigent,* crisis, emergency.

20   *do so,* do as I said.

ACT FIVE

SCENE ONE

Enter OCTAVIUS, ANTONY, *and their* Army

OCTAVIUS: Now Antony, our hopes are answered.
    You said the enemy would not come down,
    But keep the hills and upper regions.
    It proves not so; their battles are at hand;
    They mean to warn us at Philippi here,
    Answering before we do demand of them.
ANTONY: Tut, I am in their bosoms, and I know
    Wherefore they do it. They could be content
    To visit other places, and come down
    With fearful bravery, thinking by this face   10
    To fasten in our thoughts that they have courage;
    But 'tis not so.

Enter a MESSENGER

MESSENGER: Prepare you generals.
    The enemy comes on in gallant show;
    Their bloody sign of battle is hung out,
    And something to be done immediately.
ANTONY: Octavius, lead your battle softly on,
    Upon the left hand of the even field.
OCTAVIUS: Upon the right hand I, keep thou the left.
ANTONY: Why do you cross me in this exigent?   19
OCTAVIUS: I do not cross you; but I will do so.   [*March*

s.d.   Again a full martial entry.

21   *stand*, halt. *parley*, speech.

24   *answer . . . charge*, meet their attack when it comes.
25   *Make forth*, go forward.
26   *Stir . . . signal*. Octavius gives the order to his subordinates.
27 ff   This exchange of taunts and recrimination before a battle is common in Shakespeare's plays. What dramatic value has it here —to restate briefly the issues between both sides as a reminder to the audience, to work up the combatants into a pitch of anger so that the fight follows naturally, to enable the armed combatants to be easily identified in the fight to come, to show the impossibility of reconciliation?
28   *Not . . . do*. Is this a taunt of cowardice or hypocrisy?
29   *Good . . . strokes*. A jibe at Octavius' untried soldiership.
30–2   *In . . . Cæsar!* Antony fiercely compresses the two previous speeches into an attack on Brutus' treachery.
33   *The . . . unknown*, where you intend to inflict your blows is not known. The suggestion is that Antony is underhand and not to be trusted.
34–8   *But . . . sting*. The association of flattery with bees, honey and stings is illustrated in Ripa's emblem-book, *Iconologia*.
34   *Hybla bees*. The honey gathered by bees on Mt. Hybla in Sicily was famous in classical times. Cassius is sarcastically referring to Antony's 'honeyed eloquence' to the mob.
35, 36   *honeyless, stingless, soundless*. Mockingly emphatic.
37   *buzzing*, i.e. Antony's words are meaningless noise.
38   *wisely*. Sarcastic.
39   *you . . . so*, i.e. threat before striking.
41   *showed your teeth*, smiled, grinned. *fawned*. See III. i, 45–6.
45–7   *Now . . . ruled*, i.e. if Cassius' view had prevailed Antony would have died with Cæsar. See II. i, 155–61.

48   *cause*, (*a*) point, business in hand, (*b*) legal case. An image traced out in 'arguing' and 'proof'.
49   *proof*, trial by battle.

Drum. Enter BRUTUS, CASSIUS, *and their* Army; LUCILIUS,
TITINIUS, MESSALA, *and others*

BRUTUS: They stand, and would have parley.

CASSIUS: Stand fast Titinius, we must out and talk.

OCTAVIUS: Mark Antony, shall we give sign of battle?

ANTONY: No Cæsar, we will answer on their charge.
    Make forth; the generals would have some words.

OCTAVIUS: Stir not until the signal.

BRUTUS: Words before blows; is it so, countrymen?

OCTAVIUS: Not that we love words better, as you do,

BRUTUS: Good words are better than bad strokes, Octavius.

ANTONY: In your bad strokes, Brutus, you give good words:
    Witness the hole you made in Cæsar's heart,   31
    Crying 'Long live! hail Cæsar!'

CASSIUS: Antony,
    The posture of your blows are yet unknown;
    But for your words, they rob the Hybla bees,
    And leave them honeyless.

ANTONY: Not stingless too.

BRUTUS: O yes, and soundless too;
    For you have stol'n their buzzing, Antony,
    And very wisely threat before you sting.

ANTONY: Villains, you did not so, when your vile daggers
    Hacked one another in the sides of Cæsar.   40
    You showed your teeth like apes, and fawned like hounds,
    And bowed like bondmen, kissing Cæsar's feet;
    Whilst damned Casca, like a cur, behind
    Struck Cæsar on the neck. O you flatterers!

CASSIUS: Flatterers? Now Brutus thank yourself;
    This tongue had not offended so today,
    If Cassius might have ruled.

OCTAVIUS: Come, come, the cause. If arguing make us sweat,
    The proof of it will turn to redder drops.

52   *goes up*, is sheathed.

54-5   *another ... traitors*, i.e. he himself shall have been killed by the swords of the conspirators.

57   *So I hope*, i.e. that he cannot 'die by traitors' hands'.

59   *strain*, family.

61   *peevish*, silly, childish. Octavius was twenty-one years old. *worthless*, unworthy.

62   *masker*, one fond of masques. See I. ii, 203-4; II. ii, 116.

63   *Old Cassius still*, still Cassius shows the old spitefulness.

66   *stomachs*, (*a*) courage, (*b*) inclination.

S.D.   The movements of Octavius and Antony in departing should underline the defiance and contempt thrown at the conspirators.

67-8   *Why ... up*. Is this a mocking answer to Octavius or the expression of a reckless desperation?

68   *on the hazard*, at stake.

        Why does not Cassius make his confession to Brutus? Is he 'fey', wishing to justify himself, unreconciled in spirit with Brutus, ashamed, convinced of his own right judgement?

72   *as*. Restrictive use for emphasis.

75   *As Pompey was*. Pompey gave battle against his better judgement at Pharsalia where he was defeated by Julius Cæsar. *set*, stake.

77-8   *I ... opinion*, I was a strong believer in the teachings of Epicurus. Among other things the Epicureans did not believe in portents and fortune-telling by dreams.

77   *Epicurus*, a Greek philosopher (342-270 B.C.) who taught in Athens.

Look,   50
I draw a sword against conspirators;
When think you that the sword goes up again?
Never, till Cæsar's three and thirty wounds
Be well avenged; or till another Cæsar
Have added slaughter to the sword of traitors.
BRUTUS: Cæsar, thou canst not die by traitors' hands,
Unless thou bring'st them with thee.
OCTAVIUS: So I hope.
I was not born to die on Brutus' sword.
BRUTUS: O if thou wert the noblest of thy strain,
Young man, thou couldst not die more honourable.   60
CASSIUS: A peevish schoolboy, worthless of such honour,
Joined with a masker and a reveller.
ANTONY: Old Cassius still.
OCTAVIUS: Come Antony, away!
Defiance, traitors, hurl we in your teeth.
If you dare fight today, come to the field;
If not, when you have stomachs.
                    [*Exeunt Octavius, Antony, and their army*
CASSIUS: Why now, blow wind, swell billow, and swim bark.
The storm is up, and all is on the hazard.
BRUTUS: Ho Lucilius, hark, a word with you.
LUCILIUS: My lord.
                    |*Brutus and Lucilius talk apart*
CASSIUS: Messala.
MESSALA: What says my general?   70
CASSIUS: Messala,
This is my birthday; as this very day
Was Cassius born. Give me thy hand Messala.
Be thou my witness that against my will,
As Pompey was, am I compelled to set
Upon one battle all our liberties.
You know that I held Epicurus strong,

79 *partly . . . presage,* half-believe that some things do forewarn us. Cassius has become superstitious. Is this not only an omen, but perhaps an ironical echo of his accusation against Cæsar (II. i, 195)?

80 *former ensign,* foremost banner.

83 *consorted us,* accompanied us.

85 *ravens, kites.* Birds associated with death.

87 *sickly,* i.e. about to die.

88 *canopy most fatal.* Wilson notes the image is that of a dying man under a funeral canopy. *fatal,* foretelling death.

91 *fresh of spirit,* in good heart.

92 *constantly,* with determination.

93 *Even so Lucilius.* Is this conversation aside a clumsy dramatic device, or a normal issuing of orders?

94 *stand,* may they stand.

95 *Lovers,* friends.

96 *still,* ever.

97 *Let's . . . befall,* let us discuss what we shall do if the worst happens.

101 *that philosophy.* The Stoic philosophy in which suicide was considered cowardly.

102 *Cato.* See II. i, 295.

105–6 *so . . . life,* in such a way to anticipate the natural ending of life.

106 *arming,* fortifying, encouraging.

107 *To . . . powers,* to await whatever end the powers above have destined for me.

And his opinion; now I change my mind,
And partly credit things that do presage.
Coming from Sardis, on our former ensign   80
Two mighty eagles fell, and there they perched,
Gorging and feeding from our soldiers' hands,
Who to Philippi here consorted us.
This morning are they fled away and gone,
And in their steads do ravens, crows, and kites,
Fly o'er our heads, and downward look on us
As we were sickly prey: their shadows seem
A canopy most fatal, under which
Our army lies, ready to give up the ghost.
MESSALA: Believe not so.
CASSIUS: I but believe it partly,   90
For I am fresh of spirit and resolved
To meet all perils very constantly.
BRUTUS: Even so Lucilius
CASSIUS: Now most noble Brutus,
The gods today stand friendly, that we may,
Lovers in peace, lead on our days to age.
But since the affairs of men rest still incertain,
Let's reason with the worst that may befall.
If we do lose this battle, then is this
The very last time we shall speak together.
What are you then determined to do?   100
BRUTUS: Even by the rule of that philosophy
By which I did blame Cato for the death
Which he did give himself. I know not how,
But I do find it cowardly and vile,
For fear of what might fall, so to prevent
The time of life—arming myself with patience
To stay the providence of some high powers
That govern us below.
CASSIUS: Then, if we lose this battle,

187

111–   *No . . . mind.* Does Brutus renounce his principles? Wilson sug-
13   gests that as the philosopher he condemns suicide, as the Roman
       soldier faced with disgrace he sees it as the only honourable course.

113   *great*, proud, noble.

116–   *Therefore . . . made.* What movements and gestures are appro-
19   priate?

120–2 *For . . . made.* What is the effect intended by the repetition?

121   *smile*, rejoice.

123–6 *O . . . known.* Perhaps an aside. Is Brutus afraid, resigned, or fey?

The battlefield

The stage directions here and at V. iv are unusual, perhaps unique in
Shakespeare in announcing the entry of characters who left the stage at
the end of the previous scene.

Granville Barker points out the stirringly dramatic effect of the silent
stage empty for a moment, then the sudden clattering alarum—the
symbol of a battle begun.

Alternatively, movements of the soldiers and noise of battle could lead
up to the brisk urgent entry of Brutus.

1   *bills*, written orders.

2   *Unto . . . side*, i.e. to Cassius on the other wing.

3–5   *for . . . overthrow*, i.e. Octavius' forces which are facing Brutus.

4   *cold demeanour*, lack of fighting spirit, timid bearing.

You are contented to be led in triumph
Thorough the streets of Rome?   110
BRUTUS: No Cassius, no. Think not, thou noble Roman,
That ever Brutus will go bound to Rome;
He bears too great a mind. But this same day
Must end that work the ides of March begun;
And whether we shall meet again I know not.
Therefore our everlasting farewell take.
For ever, and for ever, farewell Cassius.
If we do meet again, why we shall smile;
If not, why then this parting was well made.
CASSIUS: For ever, and for ever, farewell Brutus.   120
If we do meet again, we'll smile indeed;
If not, 'tis true this parting was well made.
BRUTUS: Why then lead on. O that a man might know
The end of this day's business ere it come.
But it sufficeth that the day will end,
And then the end is known. Come ho, away!   [*Exeunt*

SCENE TWO

Alarum. Enter BRUTUS *and* MESSALA

BRUTUS: Ride, ride, Messala, ride and give these bills
Unto the legions on the other side.   [*Loud alarum*
Let them set on at once; for I perceive
But cold demeanour in Octavius' wing,

189

The battlefield

1-4   *O . . . him.* Any movements to support Cassius' words?

1   *villains*, i.e. his own men.

2   *to mine own*, against mine own men.

3   *ensign*, standard-bearer. Is the body on the stage or does Cassius enter bearing the standard?

4   *it*, standard.

7   *fell to spoil*, began to rob the defeated men.

11   *far*, farther (III. ii, 163).

19   *with a thought*, as quick as thought.

20   *get . . . hill*, i.e. to the balcony above the stage.

21   *thick*, dim.

And sudden push gives them the overthrow.
Ride, ride, Messala, let them all come down.　　　　　*[Exeunt*

SCENE THREE

Alarums. Enter CASSIUS *and* TITINIUS

CASSIUS: O look, Titinius, look, the villains fly.
　　Myself have to mine own turned enemy:
　　This ensign here of mine was turning back;
　　I slew the coward, and did take it from him.
TITINIUS: O Cassius, Brutus gave the word too early,
　　Who having some advantage on Octavius,
　　Took it too eagerly; his soldiers fell to spoil,
　　Whilst we by Antony are all enclosed.

Enter PINDARUS

PINDARUS: Fly further off my lord, fly further off;
　　Mark Antony is in your tents my lord:　　　　　　　　10
　　Fly therefore noble Cassius, fly far off.
CASSIUS: This hill is far enough. Look, look Titinius;
　　Are those my tents where I perceive the fire?
TITINIUS: They are, my lord.
CASSIUS:　　　　　　　　　Titinius, if thou lovest me,
　　Mount thou my horse, and hide thy spurs in him,
　　Till he have brought thee up to yonder troops
　　And here again, that I may rest assured
　　Whether yond troops are friend or enemy.
TITINIUS: I will be here again, even with a thought.　　*[Exit*
CASSIUS: Go Pindarus, get higher on that hill.　　　　　20
　　My sight was ever thick. Regard Titinius,
　　And tell me what thou notest about the field.　*[Exit Pindarus*

24   *where . . . end*. This thought about the completion of the circle of
life was popular. See *Coriolanus*, V. vi, 65–6; Donne, *Valediction
Forbidding Mourning*, etc.

28   *enclosed*. Perhaps a sinister word after l. 8.

31   *light*, dismount.

38   *swore . . . life*, made you take an oath as a condition of sparing your
life.

41   *Now . . . freeman*. Cassius makes Pindarus a freeman as a reward
for faithful service, and so that he may not die unworthily by the
hand of a slave. Any formal gesture to indicate the gift of freedom?

42   *search*, pierce.

44   *when . . . covered*. See III. ii, 184.

S.D.   Titinius is wearing a crown of laurels.

51   *change*, the ups and downs of fortune.

This day I breathed first: time is come round,
And where I did begin, there shall I end;
My life is run his compass. Sirrah, what news?

PINDARUS: [*Above*] O my lord!

CASSIUS: What news?

PINDARUS: [*Above*] Titinius is enclosed round about
With horsemen, that make to him on the spur,
Yet he spurs on. Now they are almost on him.   30
Now Titinius! Now some light. O he lights too.
He's ta'en. [*Shout*] And hark! they shout for joy.

CASSIUS: Come down, behold no more.
O coward that I am, to live so long,
To see my best friend ta'en before my face.

PINDARUS *descends*

Come hither sirrah.
In Parthia did I take thee prisoner,
And then I swore thee, saving of thy life,
That whatsoever I did bid thee do,
Thou shouldst attempt it. Come now, keep thine oath.   40
Now be a freeman, and with this good sword
That ran through Cæsar's bowels, search this bosom.
Stand not to answer. Here, take thou the hilts,
And when my face is covered, as 'tis now,
Guide thou the sword—Cæsar, thou art revenged,
Even with the sword that killed thee.   [*Dies*

PINDARUS: So, I am free; yet would not so have been,
Durst I have done my will. O Cassius!
Far from this country Pindarus shall run,   49
Where never Roman shall take note of him.   [*Exit*

Enter TITINIUS *and* MESSALA

MESSALA: It is but change, Titinius; for Octavius
Is overthrown by noble Brutus' power,

59   *was*. With deliberation.

64   *dangers*, i.e. the perils of the night.

65   *my success*, the result of my errand.

66   *good*. Emphasize the change in words.

67–9   *O . . . not*, i.e. melancholy men are liable to draw false and adverse conclusions.

68   *apt*, impressionable, easily deceived.

69   *soon conceived*, (*a*) quickly imagined, (*b*) easily begotten.

71   *mother*, i.e. melancholy, and hence Cassius whose melancholy mood gave birth to the error.

78   *Hie*, hasten.

81–3   *Did . . . shouts?* Is this merely to prevent the audience from being confused, or is it a sorrowful report of his errand?

As Cassius' legions are by Antony.

TITINIUS: These tidings will well comfort Cassius.

MESSALA: Where did you leave him?

TITINIUS: All disconsolate,
With Pindarus his bondman, on this hill.

MESSALA: Is not that he that lies upon the ground?

TITINIUS: He lies not like the living. O my heart!

MESSALA: Is not that he?

TITINIUS: No, this was he, Messala,
But Cassius is no more. O setting sun,   60
As in thy red rays thou dost sink tonight,
So in his red blood Cassius' day is set.
The sun of Rome is set. Our day is gone;
Clouds, dews, and dangers come; our deeds are done:
Mistrust of my success hath done this deed.

MESSALA: Mistrust of good success hath done this deed.
O hateful Error, Melancholy's child,
Why dost thou show to the apt thoughts of men
The things that are not? O Error soon conceived,
Thou never com'st unto a happy birth,   70
But kill'st the mother that engendered thee.

TITINIUS: What Pindarus! Where art thou Pindarus?

MESSALA: Seek him Titinius, whilst I go to meet
The noble Brutus, thrusting this report
Into his ears; I may say thrusting it;
For piercing steel, and darts envenomed
Shall be as welcome to the ears of Brutus
As tidings of this sight.

TITINIUS: Hie you Messala,
And I will seek for Pindarus the while.   [*Exit Messala*
Why didst thou send me forth, brave Cassius?   80
Did I not meet thy friends, and did not they
Put on my brows this wreath of victory,
And bid me give it thee? Didst thou not hear their shouts?

88   *regarded*, honoured.

89   *By . . . gods.* He seeks permission to end his life before the time
       allotted him by the gods. *part*, i.e. stage part.

93   *He is slain.* Any movement to discover the fact? How is this best
       spoken—with awe, alarm, sense of shock, bewilderment, sadness?

94–5   *O . . . abroad.* See II. i, 167–70; III. i, 270–5.

96   *proper*, own.

97   *Look . . . Cassius.* An exclamation of surprise and approval. *Look
       where*, see if, look whether.

101   *fellow*, equal.

103   *I . . . time.* To mourn or to follow Cassius' example? How should
       this be spoken?

104   *Thasos*, a Greek island not far from Philippi.

105   *funerals*, funeral ceremonies.

106   *discomfort*, depress, dishearten.

108   *battles*, troops.

110   *second fight.* According to Plutarch this occurred twenty days later.

Alas, thou hast misconstrued every thing.
But hold thee, take this garland on thy brow;
Thy Brutus bid me give it thee, and I
Will do his bidding. Brutus, come apace,
And see how I regarded Caius Cassius.
By your leave, gods—this is a Roman's part.   89
Come Cassius' sword, and find Titinius' heart.   [*Dies*

Alarum. Enter MESSALA, *with* BRUTUS, YOUNG CATO, STRATO
    VOLUMNIUS, LUCILIUS, LABEO, *and* FLAVIUS

BRUTUS: Where, where Messala, doth his body lie?
MESSALA: Lo yonder, and Titinius mourning it.
BRUTUS: Titinius' face is upward.
CATO: He is slain.
BRUTUS: O Julius Cæsar, thou art mighty yet;
  Thy spirit walks abroad, and turns our swords
  In our own proper entrails.   [*Low alarums*
CATO: Brave Titinius!
  Look where he have not crowned dead Cassius.
BRUTUS: Are yet two Romans living such as these?
  The last of all the Romans, fare thee well.
  It is impossible that ever Rome   100
  Should breed thy fellow. Friends, I owe more tears
  To this dead man than you shall see me pay.
  I shall find time, Cassius, I shall find time.
  Come therefore, and to Thasos send his body.
  His funerals shall not be in our camp,
  Lest it discomfort us. Lucilius come,
  And come young Cato, let us to the field.
  Labeo and Flavius, set our battles on.
  'T is three o'clock; and Romans, yet ere night   109
  We shall try fortune in a second fight.   [*Exeunt*

The battlefield

See note to V. ii. Is there battle action on the stage before Brutus' entry or not? Are Brutus' troops showing signs of exhaustion? Do they move in response to his encouragement?

Cato, Brutus' brother-in-law.

1–14   The arrangement and assignment of speeches here follows the Arden edition. The Folio has no stage direction after l. 1, no speech heading at l. 7, and places a speech heading *Luc.* at l. 9.

1–6   What gestures and postures are appropriate?

7–8   *And . . . Brutus.* Some editors attribute these lines to Brutus.

7–11   *And . . . son.* Lucilius, according to Plutarch, impersonated Brutus on the battlefield. Here apparently his intention is to draw the attackers away from Brutus.

9–11   How should this be grouped?

13   *There . . . straight,* there is good reason for you to kill me immediately, in that you would be killing Brutus and win honour for doing so.

Some editors insert a stage direction 'Offering money'.

16   *Room, ho!* Presumably many soldiers are crowding round.

SCENE FOUR

Alarum. Enter BRUTUS, MESSALA, YOUNG CATO, LUCILIUS,
and FLAVIUS

BRUTUS: Yet countrymen, O yet hold up your heads.   [*Exit*
CATO: What bastard doth not? Who will go with me?
  I will proclaim my name about the field.
  I am the son of Marcus Cato, ho!
  A foe to tyrants, and my country's friend.
  I am the son of Marcus Cato, ho!   [*Enter Soldiers and fight*
LUCILIUS: And I am Brutus, Marcus Brutus, I;
  Brutus my country's friend; know me for Brutus!
  O young and noble Cato, art thou down?
  Why now thou diest as bravely as Titinius,   10
  And mayst be honoured, being Cato's son.
FIRST SOLDIER: Yield, or thou diest.
LUCILIUS: Only I yield to die.
  There is so much that thou wilt kill me straight;
  Kill Brutus, and be honoured in his death.
FIRST SOLDIER: We must not. A noble prisoner.
SECOND SOLDIER: Room ho! Tell Antony, Brutus is ta'en.
FIRST SOLDIER: I'll tell the news. Here comes the general.

Enter ANTONY

  Brutus is ta'en, Brutus is ta'en my lord.
ANTONY: Where is he?
LUCILIUS: Safe Antony, Brutus is safe enough.   20
  I dare assure thee that no enemy
  Shall ever take alive the noble Brutus.
  The gods defend him from so great a shame.

25   *like himself*, true to himself, worthy of his greatness.

32   *is chanced*, turns out.
       Is Antony magnanimous, crafty, political, ostentatious, putting on a public show?

The battlefield

The entry should indicate exhausted and defeated men. Should there be any drums, trumpets or banners?

1   *remains*, survivors.
2   *Statilius . . . torch-light*. In Plutarch a scout volunteered to signal with a torch if he found all was well in the camp.

5   *in fashion*, i.e. the suicides of Cassius and Titinius.
5–8   Brutus takes each man aside in turn apart from Volumnius.

9–10 Any action expressing their horror and grief?

13   *vessel*, person.

When you do find him, or alive or dead,
He will be found like Brutus, like himself.
ANTONY: This is not Brutus, friend, but I assure you,
A prize no less in worth; keep this man safe,
Give him all kindness. I had rather have
Such men my friends than enemies. Go on,
And see where Brutus be alive or dead;   30
And bring us word unto Octavius' tent
How every thing is chanced.   [*Exeunt*

SCENE FIVE

Enter BRUTUS, DARDANIUS, CLITUS, STRATO, *and*
VOLUMNIUS

BRUTUS: Come poor remains of friends, rest on this rock.
CLITUS: Statilius showed the torch-light, but my lord,
He came not back; he is or ta'en or slain.
BRUTUS: Sit thee down, Clitus. Slaying is the word;
It is a deed in fashion. Hark thee, Clitus.   [*Whispers*
CLITUS: What I, my lord? No, not for all the world.
BRUTUS: Peace then, no words.
CLITUS: I'll rather kill myself.
BRUTUS: Hark thee, Dardanius.   [*Whispers*
DARDANIUS: Shall I do such a deed?
CLITUS: O Dardanius!
DARDANIUS: O Clitus!   10
CLITUS: What ill request did Brutus make to thee?
DARDANIUS: To kill him Clitus. Look, he meditates.
CLITUS: Now is that noble vessel full of grief,
That it runs over even at his eyes.
BRUTUS: Come thither, good Volumnius, list a word.

17–20 *The . . . come.* Why is the second visit of the ghost reported and not shown in action? Does this enhance Brutus' fortitude or standing?

18 *several,* separate.

22 *the . . . goes,* how matters are.

23 *pit,* (*a*) large hole into which animals were trapped, (*b*) grave.

26–8 *we . . . it.* Brutus appeals to Volumnius' sympathy and friendship.

29 *office,* service.

S.D. *Alarum still,* i.e. the drums and trumpet calls are increasing in intensity.

What qualities has Brutus that prevent his friends from killing him—nobility, greatness, capacity to inspire love, awesomeness?

32 *Strato . . . asleep.* Wilson notes that Shakespeare added this to show (*a*) the equanimity of Brutus, (*b*) that Strato knew nothing of his master's previous attempts at suicide.

38 *vile,* i.e. since it ends the freedom he had gained by killing Cæsar.

42 *That . . . hour.* Brutus accepts death in Stoic fashion as the winning to honourable rest.

VOLUMNIUS: What says my lord?

BRUTUS: Why this, Volumnius.
  The ghost of Cæsar hath appeared to me
  Two several times by night; at Sardis once,
  And this last night, here in Philippi fields.
  I know my hour is come.

VOLUMNIUS: Not so, my lord.   20

BRUTUS: Nay, I am sure it is, Volumnius.
  Thou seest the world, Volumnius, how it goes;
  Our enemies have beat us to the pit.   [*Low alarums*
  It is more worthy to leap in ourselves,
  Than tarry till they push us. Good Volumnius,
  Thou know'st that we two went to school together;
  Even for that our love of old, I prithee
  Hold thou my sword-hilts, whilst I run on it.

VOLUMNIUS: That's not an office for a friend, my lord.

                                          [*Alarum still*

CLITUS: Fly, fly, my lord, there is no tarrying here.   30

BRUTUS: Farewell to you; and you; and you Volumnius.
  Strato, thou hast been all this while asleep;
  Farewell to thee too Strato. Countrymen,
  My heart doth joy that yet in all my life
  I found no man but he was true to me.
  I shall have glory by this losing day,
  More than Octavius and Mark Antony
  By this vile conquest shall attain unto.
  So fare you well at once, for Brutus' tongue
  Hath almost ended his life's history.   40
  Night hangs upon mine eyes; my bones would rest,
  That have but laboured to attain this hour.

                    [*Alarum. Cry within, 'Fly, fly, fly!'*

CLITUS: Fly my lord, fly.

BRUTUS: Hence! I will follow.

                    [*Exeunt Clitus, Dardanius, and Volumnius*

203

45 *respect*, reputation.

46 *smatch*, taste, touch.

47 *turn . . . face*. See V. iii, 44.

50 *Cæsar . . . still*, i.e. Cæsar's ghost now avenged may rest.

s.D. *Alarum*. A retreat is sounded indicating that the battle is over. Then a final martial entry.

52 *What . . . that?* Is Strato standing, kneeling, with head bowed, on guard, mourning?

55 *can . . . him*, can only burn his dead body.

58-9 *so . . . true*. See V. iv, 21-2.

60 *entertain them*, take them into my service.

62 *prefer*, recommend.

67 *latest service*, i.e. honourably served him at his death.

68-75 *This . . . man!* Antony is moved to speak generously of Brutus after death. Contrast V. i, 30 ff.

71-2 *in . . . all*, out of honourable motives, and for the good of all Romans.

73 *gentle*, noble.

73-4 *elements So mixed*, his qualities so finely proportioned. See note to I. iii, 128.

I prithee Strato, stay thou by thy lord.
Thou art a fellow of a good respect;
Thy life hath had some smatch of honour in it.
Hold then my sword, and turn away thy face,
While I do run upon it. Wilt thou Strato?
STRATO: Give me your hand first. Fare you well my lord.
BRUTUS: Farewell good Strato. [*Runs on his sword*] Cæsar, now
   be still;   50
I killed not thee with half so good a will.   [*Dies*

   Alarum. Retreat. Enter OCTAVIUS, ANTONY, MESSALA,
             LUCILIUS, *and the* Army

OCTAVIUS: What man is that?
MESSALA: My master's man. Strato, where is thy master?
STRATO: Free from the bondage you are in Messala;
   The conquerors can but make a fire of him.
   For Brutus only overcame himself,
   And no man else hath honour by his death.
LUCILIUS: So Brutus should be found. I thank thee Brutus,
   That thou hast proved Lucilius' saying true.
OCTAVIUS: All that served Brutus, I will entertain them.   60
   Fellow, wilt thou bestow thy time with me?
STRATO: Ay, if Messala will prefer me to you.
OCTAVIUS: Do so, good Messala.
MESSALA: How died my master, Strato?
STRATO: I held the sword, and he did run on it.
MESSALA: Octavius, then take him to follow thee,
   That did the latest service to my master.
ANTONY: This was the noblest Roman of them all.
   All the conspirators save only he
   Did that they did in envy of great Cæsar;   70
   He only, in a general honest thought
   And common good to all, made one of them.
   His life was gentle, and the elements

79   *ordered honourably*, treated in honourable fashion, or arrayed in
      fitting manner.
80   *field*, armies.
81   *part*, share.
s.d. *Exeunt.* A funeral march or a triumphant procession?

So mixed in him that Nature might stand up
And say to all the world 'This was a man.'

OCTAVIUS: According to his virtue let us use him,
With all respect, and rites of burial.
Within my tent his bones tonight shall lie,
Most like a soldier, ordered honourably.
So call the field to rest, and let's away,   80
To part the glories of this happy day   [*Exeunt*

APPENDICES

I

THE SOURCES OF *JULIUS CÆSAR*

Julius Cæsar is derived almost entirely from Plutarch's *Lives* in the translation of Sir Thomas North, *The Lives of the Noble Grecians and Romans*, 1579, a second edition of which appeared in 1595. Appian's *Civil Wars*, published in English in 1578, may have provided hints for Antony's speech (e.g. his breaking off to weep), and for his character. Ovid's *Metamorphoses*, well known to Shakespeare both in Latin and English, may contain in Book XV the source of the account of the portents that preceded Cæsar's death, and the association of Cæsar with a star (III. i, 60–2), although similar accounts of portents occur elsewhere in Elizabethan writings. Finally the account of Cæsar added to the 1587 edition of the *Mirror for Magistrates* may have influenced slightly the incident of Artemidorus' schedule.

The historical incidents in the play cover, according to Plutarch, about three years; Shakespeare concentrates them into five days, and contrives an illusion of a close knit, swift sequence of events. Into the first day of the play are crowded several happenings distinct in time and kind: Cæsar's triumph, the Feast of the Lupercalia, and the putting to silence of Flavius and Marullus. The murder of Cæsar, the speeches in the marketplace, and the arrival of Octavius are placed on the same day, whereas in Plutarch some six weeks elapse before Octavius arrived, Brutus' speech was given on the day after the murder, and Antony's speech a day later still. Some eighteen months passed before the triumvirate of Antony, Octavius and Lepidus was formed; and about a year later at Philippi were fought the two battles which Shakespeare turns into one.

Shakespeare's knowledge of North's translation is detailed and wide-ranging; he draws material from the lives of Cæsar, Brutus, and to a lesser extent, Antony. Sometimes he incorporates passages that are close to North's. Compare the conversation between Portia and Brutus (II. i, 280–306) with the following from the Life of Brutus:

> Then perceiving her husband was marvellously out of quiet, and that he could take no rest, even in her greatest pain of all she spake in this sort unto him: 'I being, O Brutus,' said she, 'the daughter of Cato, was married unto thee; not to be thy bed-fellow and companion in bed and at board only, like a harlot, but to be partaker also with thee of thy good and evil fortune. Now for thyself, I can find no cause of fault in thee touching our match: but for my part, how may I shew my duty towards thee and how much I would do for thy sake, if I cannot constantly bear a secret mischance or grief with thee, which requireth secrecy and fidelity? I confess that a woman's wit commonly is too weak to keep a secret safely: but yet, Brutus, good education and the company of virtuous men have some power to reform the defect of nature. And for myself, I have this benefit moreover, that I am the daughter of Cato, and wife of Brutus. This notwithstanding, I did not trust to any of these things before, until that now I have found by experience that no pain or grief whatsoever can overcome me.' With those words she shewed him her wound on her thigh, and told him what she had done to prove herself. Brutus was amazed to hear what she said unto him, and lifting his hands to heaven, he besought the gods to give him the grace he might bring his enterprise to so good pass, that he might be found a husband worthy of so noble a wife as Porcia; so he then did comfort her the best he could.

At other times a word or phrase is developed into something new and important. In his account of the murder North has '. . . and among them Brutus caught a blow on his hand, because he would make one in murdering of him, and all the rest also were every man of them bloodied'. This Shakespeare has transmuted for his own purposes into the ritual bathing of the conspirators' hands in Cæsar's blood.

It is perhaps instructive to know, where so much has been drawn from Plutarch, what Shakespeare provided himself in order to glimpse his intentions: the dialogue in I. i, the swimming match between Cæsar and Cassius, Cæsar's attack of fever, Cæsar's instructions to Calphurnia at the Lupercalia, Cassius' speech on the freedom of the spirit (I. iii, 89–100),

Julius Cæsar

Brutus' speech on the oath, the nature of Calphurnia's dream, Brutus' and Antony's speeches in the market-place, Antony's description of Lepidus, the substance of the quarrel between Cassius and Brutus, the characterization of Casca, and many of the attributes of Cicero. Brutus' soliloquy (II. i, 10–34) is perhaps original, though as Schanzer notes, it may owe its 'no personal cause' to a passage in the *Comparison of Dion with Brutus*.

Even more illuminating are the alterations Shakespeare makes to the main characters as they appear in Plutarch. It is not possible in a short space to account for all the modifications, particularly as Plutarch himself is not always consistent; but some general trends are given for Cæsar and Brutus. The general picture of Cæsar is more favourable than that given by Plutarch. It is true that Shakespeare gives Cæsar physical weakness, deafness, and makes prominent his falling-sickness. On the other hand he makes Cæsar popular with the citizens not 'mortally hated'. The portents and prodigies are much enlarged as befitting Cæsar's greatness, and Cæsar's response is much more dignified and courageous; it is Calphurnia's plea that persuades him not to go to the senate—a human touch. His refusal to send a lie to the senators is not in Plutarch, nor is his setting aside with some nobility Artemidorus' schedule. His boastfulness and arrogance, his imperiousness, have been made plain, but not the rudeness with which Cæsar treated the senate in Plutarch.

Brutus, too, is more favourably presented in some respects in Shakespeare than in Plutarch, but he also is given some new failings. Plutarch describes him in glowing terms as a man of virtue and honour, given to the study of philosophy and highly regarded. He adds that he conspired against Cæsar because he wished himself to be ruler of the state, and because of some private grudge. His earlier disagreement with Cassius was due to rivalry over preferment to the office of prætor. Shakespeare sets aside these defects of character, but he imposes a rigidity of oversensitive moral principles that lead to blunders and failure. It is Brutus' fastidious moral code that leads him to reject oath taking, the political move of using Cicero or a contaminated partnership with the dissolute Antony. This lowliness and freedom from rage in Plutarch are not true of Brutus quarrelling with Cassius in the play; there he is opinionated and arrogant.

II

SHAKESPEARE'S THEATRE

ALTHOUGH the evidence for the design of Elizabethan theatres is incomplete and conflicting, the following account, it is hoped, will give a reasonable outline.

The first public theatres in London were built during Shakespeare's lifetime, but they embodied in their design and construction the experience and practice of the medieval and Tudor play productions in inn yards and elsewhere.

From square, circular or hexagonal theatre walls tiered with galleries for spectators, the Elizabethan stage jutted out over six feet above ground level and occupied about half the floor space where the spectators could stand on three sides of it. The stage of the Fortune theatre was 43 feet × 27 feet and the floor area in which it stood was 55 feet × 55 feet. At the back of the stage the lowest tier of spectators' galleries gave place to a curtained recess or inner stage used for interior scenes. On either side were dressing rooms from which entrance doors opened on to the stage. The first floor gallery behind the stage was used as a balcony for musicians or for scenes in the play; if it was not required for these purposes, spectators used it. Above the balcony and covering the rear portion of the stage was a canopy or roof painted blue and adorned with stars supported by pillars from the stage. There were trap doors in the stage and frequently a low rail around it.

The pillars, canopy, railings and back stage were painted and adorned. If a tragedy was to be performed, the stage was hung with black, but there was no set staging in the modern fashion.

There were stage properties usually of the kind that could be easily pushed on and off the stage. Records of the time mention a mossy bank, a wall, a bed, trees, arbours, thrones, tents, rock, tomb, hell-mouth, a cauldron; on the other hand pavilions and mansions may have been permanent 'sets' in some historical plays. On the whole properties were limited to essentials although the popularity of the private masques with their painted canvas sets encouraged increasing elaboration of scenery and spectacle during the reign of James I.

THE GLOBE THEATRE
A reconstruction by Dr J. C. Adams and Irwin Smith

There was no limitation to the display of rich and gorgeous costumes in the current fashion of the day. The more magnificent and splendid the better; indeed the costumes must have been the most expensive item in the requirements of the company. An occasional attempt was made at period costume, but normally plays were produced in Elizabethan garments without any suspicion of the oddness that strikes us when we read of Cæsar entering 'in his nightshirt' or Cleopatra calling on Charmian to cut the lace of what we may call her corsets. High rank was marked by magnificence of dress, a trade or calling by functional clothes. Feste, the clown, would wear the traditional fool's coat or petticoat of motley, a coarse cloth of mixed yellow and green. The coat was buttoned from the neck to the girdle from which hung a wooden dagger. Its skirts voluminous with capacious pockets in which Feste might 'impetticoat' any 'gratillity'. Ghosts, who appear in a number of plays, wore a kind of leathern smock. Oberon and magicians such as Prospero wore, in the delightful phrase and spelling of the records, 'a robe for to goo invisibell'.

The actors formed companies under the patronage of noblemen for protection against a civic law condemning them as 'rogues, vagabonds and sturdy beggars' to severe punishment. They were the servants of their patron and wore his livery. The company was a co-operative society, its members jointly owned the property and shared the profits; thus Shakespeare's plays were not his to use as he liked, they belonged to his company, the Lord Chamberlain's Men. This company, honoured by James I when it became the King's Men, was the most successful company of the period. It had a number of distinguished actors, it achieved more Court performances than any other company, and it performed in the best London theatre, the Globe, until it was burnt down during a performance of *Henry VIII* in 1613. Women were not allowed on the public stage, although they performed in masques and theatricals in private houses. Boys, therefore, were apprenticed to the leading actors and took the female parts.

The audience in the public theatres was drawn from all classes. There were courtiers and inns of court men who appreciated intricate word play, mythological allusions and the technique of sword play; there were the 'groundlings' who liked jigs, horse-play and flamboyance of speech and spectacle; and there were the citizens who appreciated the romantic stories, the high eloquence of patriotic plays and moral sentiments. A successful play would have something for all. Sometimes gallants would sit on a stool on the stage and behave rather like the courtiers in *A Midsummer Night's Dream*, V. i, or *Love's Labour's Lost*, V. ii. The 'groundlings' too were likely to be troublesome and noisy. They could buy bottled-beer, oranges and nuts for their comfort; but it is noted to their credit that when Falstaff appeared on the stage, so popular was he that they stopped cracking nuts! They applauded a well delivered speech; they hissed a boring play; they even rioted and severely damaged one theatre. Shakespeare's plays however were popular among all classes: at Court they

did so take Eliza and our James,

and elsewhere in the public theatre they outshone the plays of other dramatists. Any play of his was assured of a 'full house'. An ardent theatre-goer of the day praising Shakespeare's plays above those of other dramatists wrote:

> When let but Falstaff come,
> Hal, Poins, the rest, you scarce shall have a room,
> All is so pester'd; let but Beatrice
> And Benedick be seen, lo in a trice
> The cockpit, galleries, boxes, all are full
> To hear Malvolio, that cross-garter'd gull.

Shakespeare's Works

year of composition of only a few of Shakespeare's
can be determined with certainty. The following list
ed on current scholarly opinion.

plays marked with an asterisk were not included
First Folio edition of Shakespeare's plays (1623)
was prepared by Heminge and Condell, Shake-
's fellow actors. Shakespeare's part in them has been
debated.

2 Henry VI, 3 Henry VI.
1 Henry VI.
Richard III, Comedy of Errors.
Titus Andronicus, Taming of the Shrew, Sir
Thomas More★ (Part authorship. Four manu-
script pages presumed to be in Shakespeare's
hand).
Two Gentlemen of Verona, Love's Labour's
Lost, Romeo and Juliet, Edward III★ (Part
authorship).
Richard II, A Midsummer Night's Dream.
King John, Merchant of Venice, Love's Labour
Won (Not extant. Before 1598).
1 Henry IV, 2 Henry IV, The Merry Wives of
Windsor.
Much Ado About Nothing, Henry V.
00   Julius Caesar, As You Like It.
Hamlet, Twelfth Night.
Troilus and Cressida.
All's Well that Ends Well.

The
play
is ba
Th
in th
whic
spear
much

1590–
1591–
1592–
1593–

1594–

1595–6
1596–7

1597–8

1598–9
1599–1
1600–1
1601–2
1602–3